WALTER PATER
AN IMAGINATIVE SENSE OF FACT

Walter Pater

An Imaginative Sense of Fact

Edited by
Philip Dodd

FRANK CASS

First published 1981 in Great Britain by
FRANK CASS AND COMPANY LIMITED
Gainsborough House, 11 Gainsborough Road,
London, E11 1RS, England

and in the United States of America by
FRANK CASS AND COMPANY LIMITED
c/o Biblio Distribution Centre
81 Adams Drive, P.O. Box 327, Totowa, N.J. 07511

Transferred to Digital Printing 2004

British Library Cataloguing in Publication Data

Walter Pater.
    1. Pater, Walter – Criticism and interpretation –
Addresses, essays, lectures
    2. Authors, English – 19th century
    I. Dodd, Philip
    828'.808   PR5136

ISBN 0-7146-3183-3

This group of studies first appeared in a Special Issue
on 'Walter Pater: An Imaginative Sense of Fact' of
Prose Studies, Vol. 4, No. 1, published by Frank Cass
& Co. Ltd.

Typeset by John Smith, London

Contents

The Editor would like to thank Dr Laurel Brake for her generous
assistance with the preparation of this volume.

Notes on Contributors

Gerald Monsman   Associate Professor of English, Duke University. The author of *Pater's Portraits, Walter Pater,* and *Walter Pater's Art of Autobiography,* he has recently completed a chapter on Pater for the forthcoming book, *The Victorian Experience: The Essayists.*

Billie Andrew Inman   Professor of English, University of Arizona. Professor Inman, who has published numerous articles on Pater, is co-editor of *The Pater Newsletter,* and author of the recent book, *Pater's Reading: An Annotated Bibliography of His Library Borrowings and Literary References.*

Ian Small   Lecturer in English Literature, University of Birmingham. The editor of *The Aesthetes: A Sourcebook* and of an edition of Wilde's *Lady Windermere's Fan,* Dr Small has published a number of articles on late nineteenth-century criticism and on Pater.

Laurel Brake   Lecturer in English Literature, University College of Wales, Aberystwyth. Co-editor of *The Pater Newsletter,* and an associate editor of *The Year's Work in English Studies,* she has published articles on Victorian biography and on Pater. She is currently at work on a study of Victorian literary criticism and the periodicals.

J. B. Bullen   Lecturer in English, University of Reading. Dr Bullen has published a number of articles on Pater's interest in Renaissance art, and is the editor of a forthcoming edition of Roger Fry's *Vision and Design.* He is currently engaged on a study of the reception of Post-Impressionist painting in this country.

Sharon Bassett   Professor of English, California State University, Los Angeles. Professor Bassett has published work on Pater's connection with his intellectual milieu, and is currently participating in planning the proposed scholarly edition of the works of Walter Pater.

Robert M. Seiler   Lecturer in English Language and Literature, The University of Calgary. Dr Seiler has edited *Walter Pater: The Critical Heritage,* and is currently working on *Recollections of Walter Pater.*

Hayden Ward   Associate Professor of English, West Virginia University. The assistant editor of *Victorian Poetry,* he has published essays on Robert Browning and Robert Louis Stevenson.

Introduction
On Reading Pater

Reviewing Walter Pater's 1873 *Studies in the History of the Renaissance*, Mrs Mark Pattison complained that its title was "misleading" because "the historical element is precisely that which is wanting, and its absence makes the weak place of the whole book." The work, she found, lacked "true scientific method" and "is in no wise a contribution to the history of the Renaissance."[1] Mrs Pattison implicitly assumed here an intrinsic distinction between imaginative fiction and nonfictional prose, the latter having an obligation to convey factual material objectively. As history, Pater's *Studies* was clearly nonfiction – thus Pattisonian objectivity, prosaic and nonpoetic, must be its special form of Truth. But for Pater, prose and fiction did not deal in different sorts of truths. Taking his stance on a radical relativity (one lesson he clearly did learn from modern science), Pater denied any form of absolute or wholly objective knowledge. No historical account ever can be scientifically objective; no description ever will capture reality whole. Pater's relativistic, anti-mimetic stance grounded itself in a subjective poetics of prose which insists that all literary use of language will be self-expressive. Although Pater did not require an aesthetic response from nonliterary texts – scientific-technical writing, newspaper journalism, or 'antiquarian' research – he did imply that literary prose, like fiction, uses language expressively and imaginatively. Inevitably, Pater's self-expressive stance dictated those art-for-art's-sake (or art-for-the-artist's-sake) theories in *The Renaissance* that elevated the aesthetic-expressive qualities of language above the ostensible argument and its external referents.

One of Pater's most interesting statements concerning historical writing is found in the opening sentences of "Hippolytus Veiled", from his *Greek Studies*:

> Centuries of zealous archaeology notwithstanding, many phases of the so varied Greek genius are recorded for the modern student in a kind of shorthand only, or not at all. Even for Pausanias, visiting Greece before its direct part in affairs was quite played out, much had perished or grown dim – of its art, of the truth of its outward history, above all of its religion as a credible or practicable thing. And yet Pausanias visits Greece under conditions as favourable for observation as those under which later travellers, Addison or Eustace, proceed to Italy. ... Had the opportunities in which Pausanias was fortunate been ours, how many haunts of the antique Greek life

unnoticed by him we should have peeped into, minutely systematic
in our painstaking! how many a view would broaden out where he
notes hardly anything at all on his map of Greece![2]

One could seize on the single word, "painstaking," as a kind of clue as to
how to read the whole of this passage. In his essay on "Style," Pater
remarks that "in all science, the functions of literature reduce themselves
eventually to the transcribing of fact" and, therefore, "the excellences of
literary form in regard to science are reducible to various kinds of painstaking."[3] Pater wishes, indeed, that Pausanias had been more "painstaking" in his collection of facts. He would like to know more, but the more
he knows the more he will still want to know; he can never know enough,
can never absorb enough details to reach that point at which he can say he
has arrived at Truth.[4] Nevertheless, Pausanias' failure to perform as a
scientific historian does not prevent Pater from interpreting Greek life;
that is, scientific truth has limitations inherent in its objective mode of
explanation, such that in "Hippolytus Veiled" Pater can dispense with
factual data in his interpretation of the origin of Greek art. Even with
fuller data on the emergence of Italian renaissance art – and Pater here
longs to have for his study of Greek art the equivalent of Joseph Addi-
son's *Remarks on Italy* (1705) or J.C. Eustace's *Tour Through Italy*
(1813) – Pater does not use his facts scientifically in *The Renaissance*; he
employs corrupt texts, legends, fanciful associations. What one might
want to have in terms of historical detail is thus not what one needs to have
to re-create early Attic demi-life. To give life to an unliving past, Pater
must throw its "sensations and ideas" (the subtitle of *Marius*) into relief
against his own life; and although he gives "Hippolytus" an essay-like
subtitle, "A Study from Euripides," Pater's historical reconstruction of
the antique tragedian's tale will really veil a portrait of himself.

   Pater's shift away from the dominant Positivist-Utilitarian philosophy
of prose, away from fact and toward what he called the author's "imaginative sense of fact,"[5] constituted in 1873 a startling reaffirmation of romantic doctrine. From Sainte-Beuve, Pater had learned how inevitable was
the indirect reflection of the author himself in the style and imagery,
choice and arrangement of materials, and how inevitably criticism loses its
objectivity to become a form of creation in its own right. And out of the
nostalgia of Charles Lamb's "Dream-Children," "Mackery End," and
"Blakesmore in H----shire," Pater then crafted such subjectively confessional prose pieces as "The Child in the House." The seemingly hybrid
nature of Pater's historical novel, *Marius the Epicurean*, is immediately
resolved if one regards its hero, like Florian of "The Child in the House,"
as a sort of Elian figure designed to mask and reveal the author simultaneously. When in 1885 Pater published this work, he did so fully aware that
the current prejudice in favour of factual accuracy could be challenged by
an "imaginative sense of fact" that would be compatible with artistic
design. Utility and rhetorical fervour as Victorian prose ideals ultimately
yielded to the latent Romanticism of this expressionist mode that cele-

brated the specialness of the author's "vision within"[6] – a glimpse of the self hidden yet central to the artistic design. In all of this, Pater remains, of course, solidly imbedded in his age; for throughout the Victorian era, the utilitarian prose ideal never effectively eclipsed those uncategorizable works in which personal themes were central but submerged in the ideational content. The only reasonable explanation for history's vindication of the 'poetics' of Pater's prose is that his writings are informed by this subjective authorial presence: his unhistorical work survives whereas Mrs Pattison's voluminously documented tomes have long since been superseded in scholarly use. In the fiction of his contemporaries, Meredith and James, later in the prose and/or fiction of Yeats, Conrad, Joyce, and Woolf, Pater's ordered and delicate words, with their self-expressive intent, live.

* * *

For about a half-century, between the 1920s and the 1960s during which those born a generation or so after him were both in his debt and clamorous to deny what they owed to him, Pater's reputation was greatly diminished. The reasons had to do with the sense of nonfictional prose as a vaguely defined area, barely a literary kind at all; with the preoccupation of the dominant New Critical methodology with verse (although Pater's texts yield a wealth of meaning under close reading); and with the conflict(s) in Pater's own personality that alienated and confused readers and perhaps created personal or literary anxieties about his influence upon them. But any reader approaching Pater innocent of preconceptions would have found him, as an experimentor with problems of self and time, and as a forerunner of the twentieth-century 'psychological' novelists, considerably more than an unmarried, unchurched, prosaic version of Coventry Patmore (whose name invariably follows Pater's in alphabetical listings). Yet after the First World War it became increasingly difficult to take Pater seriously. His name seemed to elicit (at best) a mild derision – except, perhaps, from those elderly friends of one's youth who recalled his reputation from the pre-1920s. Pater was not merely neglected; he was, until the early sixties, misunderstood with wilful intent. But in the sixties, at least on the Continent and in a certain few American and British institutions, new critical methodologies better able to make sense of Pater were forged and applied (first the phenomenological method; then, later, modified and somewhat humanized versions of post-structuralism); also, sexual nonconformity was more easily introduced into open discussion and treated as a legitimate part of the author's artistic expression; and, finally, as Levine and Madden pointed out in 1968 (reviving Oliver Elton's forgotten assertion of 1920): "Victorian literature is the first for which the claim might reasonably be made that its prose non-fiction surpasses its poetry, not only in bulk but in artistic achievement."[7] (As to the reasonableness of this last, I won't take sides, since such a prose-over-poetry claim seems to consign Victorian fiction to the outermost fringes.)

Although it took fifteen years of paddling to bring Pater to shore, first against and then with the current of turning critical opinion, today his relevance and genius are past question. Yet Pater could be cited even as recently in 1975, in Miriam Allott's review of *Victorian Prose: A Guide to Research*, as " 'without a doubt the most inadequately served by biographers, scholars, and critics.' Pater is certainly the least widely read and understood of any of the Victorian critics and creative writers, though there are signs of a coming revival of interest in him; his importance in linking Victorianism and modernism is beginning to impress itself on students of both these subjects."[8] Now, a half dozen years later, it seems perfectly clear that the revaluation of his reputation and the current vigorous upsurge of Pater studies that began so tentatively in the early 'sixties has not peaked; scholarship on Pater is increasing at an exponential rate. One need only scan Robert Seiler's bibliography of Pater studies since DeLaura's *Victorian Prose* to sense an enormous activity in Pater studies in the last decade – in particular in the last two years. As a straw in the wind, the first international conference devoted exclusively to Pater was held at Brasenose College in July 1980, the essays in this special issue of *Prose Studies* representing a harvest of that gathering.

Each of the discussions included in this issue devoted to Pater touches, in some significant way, on his "imaginative sense of fact," on his struggle with the objective 'givens' of experience (ideas or individuals), and on his efforts to co-opt or turn that Other into a reordered reflection of his own image. Ian Small in a challenging essay notes that one type of critical statement Pater makes depends "upon a theory of perception and so upon a psychology of personality." Like Caesar's Gaul, all commentators on Pater find themselves divided by Small into three parts – and all alike are subjugated by "the historicist methodology." Small's own method is to propose two different models for Pater's literary and art criticism: a psychological and a sociological model. He surmises that "Pater's failure to achieve a successful synthesis of these two positions had nothing to do with the compatibility or incompatibility of the theories in themselves, but with the tensions between the opposing models of human activity from which (for the nineteenth-century mind) they derived their validation." Whatever any future discussions of Pater's sense of art as a social phenomenon (as sketched by Small) may show, the recognition of an expressive component in Pater's critical theory(ies) is sound. In the epistemology of Pater's beloved Romantic poets, the mind both is coloured by what it beholds and, in turn, colours the objects of its perception; eye and ear, says Wordsworth, "half create." Billie Andrew Inman's wide-ranging and original dissection of Pater's diverse philosophic and scientific sources for the "Conclusion" to *The Renaissance* presents just this reordering by Pater of the givens that constitutes perception as a significant act of cognition *qua* creation. Discussing a quotation from Hugo's *Les Misérables*, Inman remarks: "But as in the case of Novalis,

Pater sets the quotation from the source into a context that places a new interpretation upon it." Inman's sense of Pater's fusing or melding of scientific data to achieve his image of the gemlike flame is particularly striking. Though I myself still prefer the analogue of starlight to that of Inman's limelight (or, for that matter, to the burning glass or the Bunsen burner), the condensing and reordering of data that she adduces is certainly highly typical of Pater's method of operation and has a certain cogency. All in all, Inman cites upwards of two dozen significant influences upon the thought and imagery of the "Conclusion." What saves Pater's finale from being merely "a pastiche of other writers' ideas" is, of course, the half-creating "imaginative sense of fact" that synthesizes a divergent welter of sources into the most powerful personal manifesto of its generation.

As against the authority of a repressive parent, Pater struggled *contra* both Ruskin and Jowett. With the enormous prestige each wielded, the Slade Professor and the Master of Balliol were not unlike the empirical data of science or the authoritative philosophic and literary texts of the past. One way or another, the author who would assert his own creative originality must neutralize them. Harold Bloom has written that "Pater suffered under Ruskin's influence, though from the start he maintained a revisionary stance in regard to his precursor. ... Ruskin is ignored, by name, in the books and essays, yet he hovers everywhere in them, and nowhere more strongly than in *The Renaissance.*"[9] J.B. Bullen's essay points out that within six months of each other Ruskin and then Pater presented contrasting portraits of Michelangelo. Discussing Ruskin's "Michel Angelo and Tintoret," Bullen learnedly roots their debate over Michelangelo's place in art history in past and contemporary discussions of his reputation. Pointing to a "number of thematic similarities" in their two views, Bullen notes that Pater neither cites Ruskin nor attacks him directly; rather, Pater implicitly undermines Ruskin by presenting readers "with a different view of Michelangelo." Indeed, Pater seems to have applied against him Ruskin's very own ideas of some twenty-five years earlier: "For Pater to use an idea from Ruskin's youthful appreciation of Michelangelo so soon after the Slade lecture seems like a wry but subtle comment on Ruskin's profound change of mind about the artist."

Pater's implicit reordering of Ruskin's vision, so skilfully analyzed by Bullen, is matched by Laurel Brake's exciting use of A.C. Benson's diaries to demonstrate Pater's terrified response to Jowett's power. Everyone has long realized the trauma to Pater that the outcry over the "Conclusion" to *The Renaissance* inflicted; however, no one could have suspected, until Brake reveals it here, that, with letters supplied by Mallock, Jowett actually had *blackmailed* (that's the only word for it) Pater. Small wonder that " 'Pater's whole nature changed under the strain,' " and he became " 'old, crushed, despairing.' " In contrast to the straitened morality of Victoria's age, Pater yearned to express, both in his personal life and in his public writings, what for him had become the hallmark of the Renaissance, an unrestricted "liberty of the heart" and

"the pleasures of the senses and the imagination."[10] But having the means
to deny him this, Jowett forced Pater to put on that lifelong mask which
served to protect him equally from the hostility of critics and from those
decadent disciples who celebrated Pater's writings as the ultimate expression of art for art's sake. On a deep psychic level, the enormous need to
overturn the power of a Ruskin or a Jowett must have connected itself
with unacknowledged childhood longings for the removal of the parental
barrier and its ensuing burden of guilt at the deaths of both parents and,
later, elder brother. Yet the quotation from Henry James in Benson's
diary, uncovered by the Sherlockian sleuthing of Brake, is perhaps the
ultimate judgment by a contemporary that Pater finally was not crushed
by the 'givens' of his experience, but fought on to become a "figure" of
"strong and painful identity."

Consensus on that identity will be some time in coming, one may safely
predict. There is no sign on the horizon of a comprehensive biography of
Pater (though the sort of work that Brake is doing will certainly move it
closer), and any project to provide a scholarly edition of his works (such as
that discussed by Bassett, Seiler, and Ward) has yet to be organized.
Biographical and textual gaps leave readers ignorant in too many critical
areas of just what Pater actually did and wrote, and a clear grasp of the
personal and intellectual influences on his life and art is hampered.
Problems aplenty await future biographers and editors of his writings. The
editor of Pater's letters rather gloomily predicted that the materials for a
full-scale life may by now have irretrievably perished. Yet new material
does surface, as Brake has demonstrated. And despite its flaws, Michael
Levey's biography of a few years ago (*The Case of Walter Pater*, 1978)
helped to clarify the factual record. Indeed, perhaps a dozen or more
additional letters have turned up even after the exhaustive search that
produced Evans' *Letters of Walter Pater* (1970). The problems confronting any new edition of Pater's writings are of a related nature. Clearly any
edition would have to come to grips with that creative handling of sources
discussed by Inman, as well as with the intertwined problems of chronology and revision, symptoms also of Pater's wrestling with the priority of
the past and chastening of his psychic turmoil by elaborate orderings of
words, phrases, and whole essays. In the meantime, one very practical
undertaking might be editing several paperback selections similar to
Harold Broom's *Selected Writings of Walter Pater* (1974). Bloom's anthology is weighted toward Pater's literary criticism; other selections might
focus on art and myth, the imaginary portraits (here Eugene Brzenk's
out-of-print edition comes to mind), and the novels. These would be
feasible commercial ventures if Paterians collectively agreed to use them
in the classroom.

*   *   *

Clear agreement concerning the gaps in scholarly spadework that the
future must fill is somewhat diminished in the critical sphere by the large
number of options. Generally speaking, the future of Pater criticism may

very well lie in all those interrelationships, outward from his autobiographical impulse to the other texts of his era, inward from the links
between his style and topics to the depths of his psyche. Shifts in the
reputation or disagreements about the status of particular works perhaps
will concern the future reader less than the potential of almost any work to
reveal what James calls Pater's "strong and painful identity." To illustrate
the potential for the sort of relatively unexplored close readings in which
future criticism may well excel, I would like to offer a single paragraph in
"Hippolytus Veiled" for consideration. As a Greek study, it obviously has
in common with the Renaissance studies a historical foundation; and, also
in common with them, it is concerned with "what irresistible fancy super-
induces on historic details, themselves meagre enough."[11] Following a
long (approximately one quarter the total length of the study) Sainte-
Beuve style preamble or overture with its reflections on new art and old
religion, Pater moves to the myth of Hippolytus, introducing first Theseus
and the rape of Antiope, then turning wholly to what "irresistible fancy"
adds over and above the recorded facts: a paragraph describing how the
rejection of mother and child by the father is replaced by a new found
mother-son relationship wherein the son as consort will fulfil the role of
the father. Though longish, the paragraph should be given in full:

In one of these doomed, decaying villages, then, King Theseus
placed the woman and her babe, hidden, yet secure, within the Attic
border, as men veil their mistakes or crimes. They might pass away,
they and their story, together with the memory of other antiquated
creatures of such places, who had had connubial dealings with the
stars. The white, paved waggon-track, a by-path of the sacred way to
Eleusis, zigzagged through sloping olive-yards, from the plain of
silvered blue, with Athens building in the distance, and passed the
door of the rude stone house, furnished scantily, which no one had
ventured to inhabit of late years till they came there. On the ledges
of the grey cliffs above, the laurel groves, stem and foliage of
motionless bronze, had spread their tents. Travellers bound north-
wards were glad to repose themselves there, and take directions, or
provision for their journey onwards, from the highland people, who
came down hither to sell their honey, their cheese, and woollen
stuff, in the tiny market-place. At dawn the great stars seemed to
halt a while, burning as if for sacrifice to some pure deity, on those
distant, obscurely named heights, like broken swords, the rim of the
world. A little later you could just see the newly opened quarries,
like streaks of snow on their russet-brown bosoms. Thither in
spring-time all eyes turned from Athens devoutly, intent till the first
shaft of lightning gave signal for the departure of the sacred ship to
Delos. Racing over those rocky surfaces, the virgin air descended
hither with the secret of profound sleep, as the child lay in its cubicle
hewn in the stone, the white fleeces heaped warmly round him. In
the wild Amazon's soul, to her surprise, and at first against her will,

the maternal sense had quickened from the moment of his conception, and (that burst of angry tears with which she had received him
into the world once dried up), kindling more eagerly at every token
of manly growth, had at length driven out every other feeling. And
this animal sentiment, educating the human hand and heart in her,
had become a moral one, when, King Theseus leaving her in anger,
visibly unkind, the child had crept to her side, and tracing with small
fingers the wrinkled lines of her woebegone brow, carved there as if
by a thousand years of sorrow, had sown between himself and her
the seed of an undying sympathy.[12]

Considered as an instance of the handling of language, this passage is
remarkable for its rhythm and sound as well as for the precise details that
delineate feelings (Pater's "you" firmly placing the reader). It opens with
a sinister alliteration of "doomed, decaying" and closes with the tender
sibilance of the S-Os in an iambic diminuendo: "ǎ thǒusǎnd yéars ǒf
sórrǒw, hǎd sǒwn bětwéen hǐmsélf ǎnd hér thě sěed ǒf ǎn ǔndýǐng sým-
pǎthy," the accent falling heavily on the alliterating words which are also
the main carriers of the thought – sorrow [had] sown [the] seed [of]
sympathy. The effulgent landscape contrasting with the stars in the darkness just before dawn echoes the other major contrast of hard stone with
tender maternal love. The dominant imagery is lapidary (as it is of the
whole story, since Hippolytus dies on the rocks): "the rude stone house,"
"the grey cliffs," "those distant, obscurely named heights, like broken
swords, the rim of the world," "the newly opened quarries," the "rocky
surfaces" over which the virgin air races, the child's "cubicle hewn in the
stone," the "carved" lines of the mother's brow. Contrasting with the
harsh glare and hard stone is the tenderness of the mother-child sentiment, associated with images of rest, protection, and nourishment: the
travellers who "repose themselves" and buy from the highlanders "their
honey, their cheese, and woollen stuff, in the tiny market-place"; or the
sleeping child with "the white fleeces heaped warmly round him"; or the
pervasive images of renewal – the stars at dawn, the sacred ship in
springtime, the newly opened quarries, and the sowing of the "seed" of
sympathy. The contrast actually becomes an exchange of qualities as the
rocky heights, humanized by Antiope's new found maternity, are
described as having "bosoms" and Antiope, assuming something of their
monumental endurance, is presented with her brow "carved" like marble.
Finally, the "newly opened quarries," hinting at the burgeoning of Greek
statuary and art, parallel the quickening of Antiope's maternal instinct,
the opening of the "heart in her."
The emotional core of this paragraph is a set of negative and positive
familial relationships (lust, betrayal, hate; pity, love, worship) that in this
story are simultaneously present in their maternal and paternal enuncia-
tion. Thus the ambivalent Artemis, implicitly present in the "great stars"
and Arcadian mountains, incorporates in her person the antagonistic
mothers, Phaedra and Antiope – a dialectic doubled elsewhere in the

Greek Studies volume in the relation of Demeter to her daughters, Perse-phone and Kore. The paternal conjugates in the narrative are more complexly and provocatively related than the mothers. If Theseus is the father who, like Phaedra, destroys Hippolytus, then the *pater* who, like Antiope, sympathizes with Hippolytus is Pater. Just as Artemis in her person blends the figures of Phaedra and Antiope, so the text itself subsumes the figures of Theseus and Pater. But it is immediately evident that Pater is not a figure in the plot quite like Phaedra, Antiope, or Theseus; he belongs to the enclosing border, to the authorial level of inscription. The essence of Pater's thinking about textuality, however, involves precisely this reflexive or specular relation between inner and outer levels of plot and inscription. Expressed as a literary 'proportion,' the relationships would be: Artemis is to Antiope-Phaedra as Pater is to Pater-Theseus. Within the plot, Pater, the son who in biographical fact lost his father, exists as Hippolytus, the son rejected by the absent father. This Pater is merely the "painstaking" reconstructor of Euripides' lost drama, a victim of the literary past that denies him originating potency. Merely a son, his name mocks him as a father. But outside the plot, Pater establishes himself by the authorial act of inscription as precisely that authority figure (author, authority: same root) against which the young Hippolytus (like the young Pater against Ruskin or Jowett) struggled. Through an extended act of recreative writing, Pater recovers Euripides' *Hippolytus Veiled* to become the originating father of "Hippolytus Veiled."

But this authorial paternity is ambivalent. The desired authority *vis-à-vis* the now-subjected past is established, but simultaneously the future turns towards Pater-Theseus the face of a potential rival. Pater-Theseus now seeks to deny Antiope's recognition (in the sentence that serves as the transition into the quoted paragraph) "that a male child might be the instrument of her anger, and one day judge her cause." Hippolytus, to whom the father has become a villain – " a vile little opportunist," as Benson characterized Jowett – is about to replace Theseus by becoming the consort of the mother. The child, "tracing with small fingers the wrinkled lines of her woebegone brow," recalls both the Christ child of Botticelli's Madonna del Magnificat, who in Pater's *Renaissance* "guides" his mother's "hand to transcribe in a book the words of her exaltation,"[13] and also the hero of Pater's novel, who takes dictation from his dying friend – Flavian's "sharply contracted hand in the hand of Marius."[14] The sorrowing "lines" of Antiope's brow, "the high cold words" of the Madonna's book, the fevered stanzas of the dying Flavian's poem – in each instance the elder 'parental' figure is displaced by the younger as the inscriber of the text. Although Theseus hopes that Antiope and Hippol-ytus "might pass away, they and their story," he cannot so easily "veil" his "crimes." When Hippolytus replaces the father to become his mother's consort, Theseus will be denied originating paternity – veiled, ironically, as his own victim. Artemis remains, then, as the only power not subject to displacement; she is the ultimate origin. As a goddess who presides over the text in which Pater is so ambiguously implicated, she is allied to a host of similar figures in Pater's writings, most notably the Mona Lisa, who elsewhere (in *Walter Pater's Art of Autobiography*) I have termed an "angel of art." Throughout the corpus of Pater's writings, this flux-ruling angel recurs, appearing, for example, in the portrait of Winckelmann in *The Renaissance* as the sinister Arcangeli ("Mr. Archangels") who slays Winckelmann at his moment of crowning authorial glory, but also appearing benignly in an earlier chapter as Pico coming to Ficino on the very day the latter completed his life's work, the translation of Plato into Latin (becoming, like Pater redoing Euripides into English, the Latin father of the Greek Plato). Pico is presented here as "a young man, not unlike the archangel Raphael," an incarnation of "inward harmony and completeness."[15]

Standing outside or above or beyond any finite set of boundaries, this Artemis is the textual goddess Pater, too, worships. Although a 'reading' such as this seems to pull together the hints and surmises that scholarship and criticism up till now have supplied, it is only one possible psychic profile for the elusive Walter Pater. There will certainly be others as the interpretive pattern grows in complexity and interest from dimension to dimension. The first fugitive hints seem now like a mere line; the more sophisticated discussions in the last ten or fifteen years are, by contrast, perhaps like a square. But the insight of the future may well be like a cube – some act of scholarship or criticism revealing a texture and tone in Pater's imaginative sensibility as yet unimagined and unimaginable.

GERALD MONSMAN
Duke University

NOTES

1. E.F.S. Pattison (Mrs Mark Pattison), "Art," review of several volumes, including *Studies in the History of the Renaissance*, by Walter Pater, *The Westminster Review*, NS 43 (1873), 639-40.
2. *Greek Studies: A series of Essays* (London: Macmillan, 1910), pp.152-3.
3. *Appreciations, with an Essay on Style* (London: Macmillan, 1910), p.9.
4. See Gerald Monsman, *Walter Pater* (Boston: G.K. Hall, 1977), pp.60-2.
5. *Appreciations*, p.8.
6. *Appreciations*, p.9.
7. "Introduction," in *The Art of Victorian Prose*, ed. George Levine and William Madden (New York: Oxford U.P., 1968), p.xvii. In *A Survey of English Literature 1830-1880*, Oliver Elton writes: "if we leave aside the distinction between pure and applied literature, and simply weigh the prose of the time against the verse, it would seem that while there is a great and noble body of achievement in verse, the achievement of prose, both in range and quality, is greater still." Quoted in "Introduction," in *Prose of the Victorian Period*, ed. William Buckler (Cambridge: The Riverside Press, 1958), p.xi.
8. Miriam Allott, review of *Victorian Prose: A Guide to Research*, ed. David DeLaura, *Victorian Studies*, 19 (1975), 109.
9. "Introduction," in *Selected Writings of Walter Pater*, ed. Harold Bloom (New York: The New American Library, 1974), pp.xv-xvi.

10. *The Renaissance: Studies in Art and Poetry* (London: Macmillan, 1910), p. 24.
11. *Greek Studies*, p. 158.
12. *Greek Studies*, pp. 163-4.
13. *Renaissance*, p. 57.
14. *Marius the Epicurean: His Sensations and Ideas* (London: Macmillan, 1910), I, 118.
15. *Renaissance*, p. 37.

The Intellectual Context of Walter Pater's "Conclusion"

For eight years before Pater wrote the conclusion to "Poems by William Morris," the first version of the "Conclusion" to *The Renaissance*, his mind had been selecting and storing ideas, images, and techniques that would come together in the composition of this work. Readings in philosophy and Goethe dating 1860-3, readings in aesthetics and Renan dating 1863-5, and recent readings in belles lettres and contemporary science – all came to bear upon this brief conclusion.

The immediate inspiration for the "Conclusion" was very likely Morris' *Earthly Paradise*, Parts I and II of which (March-August) had appeared in April of 1868 and which Pater was reviewing. On its face, in its original context, the "Conclusion" is a defence of Morris' new, un-utilitarian poetry. Moreover, the comprehensive theme of the "Conclusion" could have been derived from *The Earthly Paradise*. As a reviewer, Pater discerned in this work a dominant theme that he was able to empathize with, and which he expressed in the review in one of his very best phrases: "the desire of beauty, quickened by the sense of death."[1] The "Conclusion" is his own elaboration upon this theme: the first half evokes the sense of death, the second half the desire of beauty quickened by the sense of death. In addition, the persona in the "Conclusion" is in some respects like the Wanderers in Morris' poem, who learn from their long wandering that the earthly paradise they have sought does not exist and that they cannot escape death. At the end of the quest, a remnant of these men arrive at "a nameless city in a distant sea." After describing many of their experiences for the Elders of the city, their spokesman states their primary discovery – that "the lot of all men should be ours / A chequered day of sunshine and of showers / Fading to twilight and dark night at last."[2] As the Wanderers contemplate the remainder of their lives, it is as if they say, as Pater does in the last paragraph of his review, "we have an interval and then we cease to be"; how can we "make as much as possible of the interval?" (312) Like Pater's "wisest" people, they choose to spend the interval, in part, "in art and song," retelling stories from their native lands, but with an awareness of death that makes every pleasure exquisitely melancholy. In other words, the dilemma of the persona in the "Conclusion" and the resolution of the dilemma echo the dilemma of the Wanderers and its resolution. The Apology of *The Earthly Paradise* recommends to readers, who are assumed to be in a similar dilemma, a similar resolution:

> But rather, when aweary of your mirth,
> From full hearts still unsatisfied ye sigh,
> And, feeling kindly unto all the earth,
> Grudge every minute as it passes by,
> Made the more mindful that the sweet days die –
> – Remember me a little then I pray,
> The idle singer of an empty day.

Pater's "Conclusion" might be called a brilliant elaboration upon Morris' theme – "Grudge every minute as it passes by / Made the more mindful that the sweet days die." But the appeal for readers of Pater is not so much in the theme itself as in the texture of the elaboration and the rich and complex intellectual context that informs it, the context that this paper proposes to elucidate.

The first half of the "Conclusion" (the first four paragraphs in the 1868 version), which creates the sense of death, is not a continuous argument. It is two discourses, each with its beginning and end, the first derived from contemporary science and the second from sceptical philosophy. Anyone who approaches the first half as if it were one argument and begins a close analysis of its logic will soon discern a central inconsistency: the persona speaks authoritatively in the first paragraph about the constitution of the physical world and the unity of humanity with the physical world; but in the second and third paragraphs, he denies knowledge of the physical world and proclaims the isolation of the individual person. For example, the most recent critic to analyze the 'argument,' Perry Meisel, soon discovers "blindness" and "deception" in Pater's mind. Summarizing the logical problem, he states:

> If experience is ringed round by personality, where is the 'without' from which forces are supposedly to pass through it? Indeed, nothing at all is supposed to be able to pierce the individual ringed round in his 'isolation' (R, 215), even though such a claim requires for its own coherence some notion of an inside and an outside clearly separated from one another. Pater's solipsism, in other words, is erected on a spatial metaphor whose truth he is here intent to deny as he requires it in order to deny it.[8]

What Meisel does not see is that Pater is representing "modern thought" in the first half of the "Conclusion," as he says in the first sentence. He is saying that whether we "begin with that which is without," as modern science does, or "begin with the inward world of thought and feeling," as modern philosophy does, we become equally disillusioned, because neither gives us any basis for metaphysical certainty. Both approaches cast us into flux, depressing us with the sense of death. In short, Pater is saying that whether we turn to science or philosophy, however different their assumptions and approaches may be, we do not find an assuring presence.

I have three reasons for saying that Pater was influenced by contemporary science in the writing of the first paragraph of the "Conclusion." First, he refers to science by name in the text, twice. Second, he imitates the style of scientific demonstration, using the imperative "Let us begin" and "Fix upon it"; the second person plural pronoun; the present tense of verbs; and many common concrete nouns. All of these techniques had been used together repeatedly in scientific writing from Bacon's to Tyndall's. Third, the concept developed in the first paragraph was one of the leading conclusions of biological scientists working in the late 1860s, the physical basis of life, or the absence of any force but chemical forces in all of life's processes, including thought. This concept was powerfully presented by George Henry Lewes in an article that appeared in the avant-garde *Fortnightly Review* at the beginning of the month in which Pater completed his review on Morris, July 1868.[4] It was the third part in a four-part essay entitled "Mr. Darwin's Hypotheses."[5] Although there is no external evidence that Pater read this article, the issue of the *Fortnightly* in which it appeared also contained Swinburne's "Notes on Designs of the Old Masters at Florence,"[6] which nobody doubts that Pater read. Lewes had informed himself about cell life by reading Max Schultze and other German cytologists, and in the first several pages of this essay he discusses their findings. His opening sentence must have been fascinating to contemporary readers: "The simplest form of organic life is not – as commonly stated – a cell, but a microscopic lump of jelly-like substance, or protoplasm" (61). But his biggest news was that a cell is " 'a nucleus with surrounding protoplasm' " (61). Earlier in the nineteenth century protoplasm had been associated with cells, but that it was the essential environment of the nuclei of all cells had not been assumed.[7] Lewes summarizes the leading scientific conception of existence in nature, stating: "Every individual object, organic or inorganic, is the sum of two factors: – first, the relation of its constituent molecules to each other; secondly, the relation of its substance to all surrounding objects" (62). He explains that every cell has a life cycle of its own: "it is born, is developed, and decays" (62). After discussing cells in relation to lower forms of life, he turns to higher forms, using the following web image, somewhat similar to Pater's "strange perpetual weaving and unweaving of ourselves" (311): "Rising still higher, we see animal forms of which the web is woven out of myriads upon myriads of cells, with various cell-products, processes, fibres, tubes" (62).

If Pater read Lewes' article in July 1868, it could have acted as a prompter, but it probably did not introduce him to the idea that the physical constituents of the human body are constantly changing and that they are integral to a larger physical system. Herbert Spencer had already expressed these ideas in *The Principles of Biology*, 1864-7,[8] although he was apparently unaware of the significance of protoplasm to cell life. It is uncertain whether Pater read Spencer, but the conceptual and verbal parallels between Spencer's text and Pater's make it seem likely that he did. Spencer discusses at length the chemical elements that compose organic matter; he discusses "the unceasing change of matter which oxygen and other agents produce throughout the system"; and he discusses "certain molecular re-arrangements of an unstable kind."[9] He summarizes his description of organic change, as follows:

> Thus we have growth, decay, changes of temperature, changes of consistence, changes of velocity, changes of excretion, all going on in connexion; and it may be as truly said of a glacier as of an animal, that by ceaseless integration and disintegration it gradually undergoes an entire change of substance without losing its individuality. (I, 67)

Spencer's very assurance that individuality is preserved in spite of change might have implanted a fear that inspired Pater's image, in the fourth paragraph, of a person "losing even his personality, as the elements of which he is composed pass into new combinations" (311).

At one point the verbal similarity between Pater's text and Spencer's is striking. In the sixth sentence, Pater states: "Our physical life is a perpetual motion of them [elements in process] – the passage of the blood, the wasting and repairing of the lenses of the eye" (310). Spencer's Chapter 4 in Volume I is entitled "Waste and Repair," and one lengthy paragraph is concerned with the eye, or specifically the simultaneous waste and repair of vision (173-4). Another verbal parallel, "from moment to moment," occurs in passages that deal with heat. Pater states:

> This at least of flame-like our life has, that it is but the concurrence renewed from moment to moment of forces parting sooner or later on their ways. (310)

Spencer had stated:

> There can be no doubt that this thermal re-action which chemical action from moment to moment produces in the body, is from moment to moment an aid to further chemical action. (I,45)

If Pater did not read Lewes and Spencer, it is plain that he had acquired scientific information like theirs somewhere, and it is interesting to observe that in handling scientific matter, he was careful to follow a principle enunciated by Hegel in the *Ästhetik*, which he had borrowed from the Queen's College Library, 28 April – 23 May, 1863.[10] In the *Ästhetik*, Hegel distinguishes between the scientist's mode of thinking, and the artist's, stating, "the beauty of art is presented to sense, feeling, perception, and imagination: its field is not that of thought, and the comprehension of its activity and its creations demands another faculty than that of scientific intelligence."[11] Pater had applied Hegel's distinction previously. In "Coleridge's Writings," he praises Wordsworth for expressing as a sentiment his conception of an intelligence in nature, in a manner "which perfect art allows" (in other words, which perfect art allows, according to Hegel), while criticizing Goethe for expressing a similar idea in "Gott and Welt" in technical, scientific language, which he says is "something stiffer than poetry."[12] He was to apply it again, in 1869, in "Notes on Leonardo da Vinci," in saying: "Goethe himself reminds one how great for the artist may be the danger of over-much science ... he did not invariably find the spell-word, and in the second part of *Faust*, presents us with a mass of science which has no artistic character at all."[13] True to Hegelian principle, Pater, in the first paragraph of the "Conclusion," avoids Goethe's 'mistake': his technique is to hold scientific detail to a minimum and to use a maximum of metaphor, even though he is stating scientific conclusions and suggesting the authoritative style of scientific demonstration.

As Pater turned inward in the second paragraph of the "Conclusion," he was, as far as sources are concerned, moving backwards in time. The undergraduate register at the Queen's College Library shows that Pater pursued a self-formed course of reading in philosophy beginning in November 1860 and ending in December 1863. The first philosophical book borrowed was Volume II of Fichte's *Werke*, containing *Darstellung der Wissenschaftslehre (The Science of Knowledge), Die Bestimmung des Menschen (The Vocation of Man),* and other works. He proceeded from Fichte to Hobbes, to Ritter's *History of Ancient Philosophy* in Alexander J.W. Morrison's translation, to Hume, Kant, Schleiermacher, Reid, Berkeley, Bacon, Locke, Hegel, Lucretius, Plato's *Theætetus*, Fichte again (this time, Volume V of the *Werke*, including *Versuch einer Kritik aller Offenbarung (Essay toward a Critique of All Revelation), Die Anweisung zum seligen Leben (The Way towards the Blessed Life)*, and other works), *Theætetus* again, and, finally, Eduard Zeller's *Die Philosophie der Griechen*. In his reading Pater encountered a number of times the sceptical argument stated in the "Conclusion." That it had an impact upon him is indicated in "The History of Philosophy," unpublished manuscript No. 3 in the collection at the Houghton Library, Harvard University.[14] In this manuscript, Pater explains the effect that reading philosophy has on a young truth-seeker. He states that the first step in the intellectual quest is always scepticism, and as philosophers who introduce the neophyte to scepticism, he lists Fichte, Berkeley, Spinoza, and Kant, in that order. At another point in the manuscript he lists as milestones of modern scepticism "Berkeley's Theory of Vision, Kant's Criticism, and Fichte's _____." That Pater did not remember the name of Fichte's book is not very significant, since he often left blanks where names and specific examples were needed. What is significant is that Fichte appears, with Berkeley and Kant, in both lists. Add to this prominence the fact that Fichte came first in the order of reading in 1860, and it is easy to conclude that Pater made his first step in the philosophical search, the step toward scepticism, while reading Fichte. Internal evidence also points to Fichte as the primary influence. Pater's explanation of the sceptical argument in the second and third paragraphs of the "Conclusion" bears more resemblance to Fichte's in *The Vocation of Man* than to that of any other philosopher. The book as a whole follows the course of one neophyte's quest for truth, from the first stirring of the philosophic impulse to the final resolution in faith. It is divided into three parts: "Doubt," "Knowledge," and "Faith." The theme of the perpetual flux is developed in

"Doubt," with an emphasis, like Pater's, on moments that pass so rapidly that they can never be said to *be*. For example, Fichte has his neophyte say: "Nature pursues her course of ceaseless change, and while I yet speak of the moment which I sought to detain before me it is gone, and all is changed; and in like manner, before I had fixed my observation upon it, all was otherwise."[15] Near the end of the section called "Knowledge," Fichte explains the impossibility of knowing anything by empirical means. The first sentence states the main theme of the second and third paragraphs of the "Conclusion," and even suggests the organization of the first half of the whole:

> There is nothing enduring, either out of me, or in me, but only ceaseless change. I know of no being, not even of my own. There is no being. I myself absolutely know not, and am not. Pictures are: – they are the only things which exist, and they know of themselves after the fashion of pictures: – pictures which float past without there being anything past which they float; which, by means of like pictures, are connected with each other: – pictures without anything which is pictured in them, without significance and without aim. I myself am one of these pictures: – nay, I am not even this, but merely a confused picture of these pictures. All reality is transformed into a strange dream, without a life which is dreamed of, and without a mind which dreams it; – into a dream which is woven together in a dream of itself. Intuition is the dream; thought, – the source of all the being and all the reality which I imagine, of my own being, my own powers, and my own purposes, – is the dream of that dream. (I, 402)

The idea here that nothing exists but pictures in the mind is paralleled by Pater's "swarm of impressions," "unstable, flickering, inconsistent, which burn, and are extinguished with our consciousness of them" (310); his idea that the pictures float is paralleled by Pater's "race of the midstream" and his image of an impression as "a tremulous wisp constantly reforming itself on the stream";[16] and the dream imagery is paralleled by Pater's famous idea that each mind keeps "as a solitary prisoner its own dream of a world" (311). Fichte's description of the solipsistic mind is enhanced by the following additional statement: "Not immediately from thee to me, nor from me to thee, flows forth the knowledge which we have of each other – we are separated by an insurmountable barrier" (I, 460). In Pater's text the barrier is called "that thick wall of personality through which no real voice has ever pierced on its way to us, or from us to that, which we can only conjecture to be without" (310).

That the sceptical argument had a peculiar fascination for Pater is suggested by the fact that when explaining scepticism in *The Vocation of Man*, Fichte was trying to discredit it. To him the solipsistic state to which scepticism led was so absurd as to prompt a new approach to the whole question of truth, which he pursued in "Faith." Whether Pater was initially persuaded by Fichte's basis for faith is an open question, but that he rejected it at some point is obvious from statements in "The History of Philosophy." In this manuscript Pater says that even though scepticism seems fantastic to most people, it is "the dominion of the common sense for all really instructed minds." And, further, "The mind which has once broken the smooth surface of what seemed its self-evident principles can never again be as natural as a child's, nor perhaps will it ever find an equivalent for its earlier untouched healthfulness in that rationalised conception of experience, and man's relation to it, by which it is the ambition of philosophy to replace it."

Less pervasive influences on the second and third paragraphs of the "Conclusion" than Fichte's very likely came from Hume, Berkeley, and Plato. Hume's influence can be seen in Pater's repeated use of the term *impressions*, instead of Berkeley's *sensations*, and Fichte's *pictures*. The term *infinitely divisible*, used in the third paragraph of the "Conclusion," perhaps also came from Hume. Pater states: "Analysis goes a step further still, and tells us that ... each of them [impressions of the individual] is limited by time, and that as time is infinitely divisible, each of them is infinitely divisible also" (311). This seems to be what Pater understood from Hume's Sections I and II in Part II of Book I of *A Treatise of Human Nature*, entitled "Of the Infinite Divisibility of Our Ideas of Space and Time" and "Of the Infinite Divisibility of Space and Time," respectively. If these two chapters were the source, however, Pater misinterpreted Hume or disagreed with him. Hume had taken up the subject of infinite divisibility of time in order to deny it, assuming that time had to be made up of indivisible parts, or there could be no progression. He states: "For if in time we could never arrive at an end of division, and if each moment, as it succeeds another, were not perfectly single and indivisible, there would be an infinite number of co-existent moments, or parts of time; which I believe will be allow'd to be an arrant contradiction."[17] For Hume, infinite divisibility was identical with "a total annihilation," which he rejected (27). Of course, Pater could simply have been presenting the point of view of Aristotle, who said in the *Physics*: "every line is divided *ad infinitum*. Hence it is so with time."[18] It is important to note, however, that Pater absorbed Hume's distinctive and central idea (recreated derisively by Fichte in his rendering of the sceptical stance) that the mind is only a collection of perceptions, in constant motion. Hume states in the *Treatise*: "But setting aside some metaphysicians of this kind [who maintain that they perceive something simple and continuous that they call themselves], I may venture to affirm of the rest of mankind, that they are nothing but a bundle or collection of different perceptions, which succeed each other with an inconceivable rapidity, and are in a perpetual flux and movement" (252).

Berkeley's influence can be seen specifically in the following passage: "when reflection begins to act upon those objects [which surround the perceiver] they are dissipated under its influence, the cohesive force is suspended like a trick of magic, each object is loosed into a group of impressions, colour, odour, texture, in the mind of the observer" (310).

Although Hume referred to senses other than sight in a general way, it was Berkeley who repeatedly referred to sensations from the other senses, as well as to colour in visual sensations.[19]

Plato influenced the "Conclusion" in two ways, the first of which was indirect. Reading Plato's *Theætetus*, with marginal summaries and copious notes in Lewis Campbell's eloquent English, in March 1863, must have been an awakening experience for Pater.[20] Here, in this ancient text, he found concepts that he had thought to be modern: such as, relativity, the perpetual flux, and the subjectivity of knowledge. The Pythagorean argument detailed in this dialogue must have seemed like a review of the sceptical ideas that he had previously found in modern sources. He concluded, as he states in "History of Philosophy," that "successive metaphysical systems have been, in fact, little more than so many recombinations of the pieces which Plato had long ago placed, once for all upon the board." The indirect influence of Plato's *Theætetus*, then, was to confirm sceptical ideas that Pater had already absorbed from other sources. One passage in the "Conclusion," however, which seems not to have been anticipated in any of the other sources that Pater had read, could have been inspired directly by a passage in *Theætetus*. Pater refers to objects, not "in the solidity with which language invests them, but of impressions unstable, flickering, inconsistent" (310). The reference seems to echo the following passage from Section 157 of *Theætetus*:

> there arises a general reflection, that there is no one self-existent thing, but everything is becoming and in relation; and being must be altogether abolished, although from habit and ignorance we are compelled even in this discussion to retain use of the term. But great philosophers tell us that we are not to allow either the word 'something,' or 'belonging to something,' or 'to me,' or 'this' or 'that,' or any other detaining name to be used; in the language of nature all things are being created and destroyed, coming into being and passing into new forms; nor can any name fix or detain them.[21]

Thus, what appears to be in Pater's text an anticipation of an idea current in modern semantics – that language creates an illusion of solidity and certainty – could easily have been derived from Plato, who regarded it as already established by other philosophers.

In sum, in the first half of the "Conclusion" Pater shows that modern science can only integrate the human being into the chemical universe and that philosophy, when it presumes to convey truth and is "sincere" ("William Morris," 309), can only consign the human mind to a solipsistic isolation. These are the "truths" that "the modern world is in possession of," to which Pater had referred contemptuously in the paragraph preceding the conclusion to "William Morris" – truths that do not make the spirit free but overwhelm it with the sense of death. In the second half of the "Conclusion" Pater tries to circumvent science and philosophy by simulating a return to an earlier mental state, or, as he calls it in "The History of Philosophy," an "unreflecting" and "unsuspecting receptivity of mind." He has accepted the idea of eventual dissolution, the truth of science, and the subjectivity of knowledge, the truth of philosophy; but he endeavours to compensate for them through intensity of consciousness, and he subdues philosophy to his own purpose by making it an agent in the process of perceiving.

Pater knew at the time he was writing *Marius the Epicurean* that the experiential stance, which he had created in the second half of the "Conclusion," did not necessarily follow from the metaphysical propositions of the flux and the subjectivity of knowledge, which he had laid down in the first half;[22] and he probably knew this when he wrote the "Conclusion." Two philosophers with whom he was familiar had preceded him in assuming an experiential ethic after stating a sceptical philosophical position – David Hume and Aristippus of Cyrene, Hume by simply circumventing scepticism of the senses and Aristippus by apparently "deducing" the experiential ethic from the sceptical base. It is significant that Pater did not list Hume in "The History of Philosophy" among the philosophers who led the neophyte into scepticism, even though he must have known that Hume was recognized in the history of philosophy as a leading sceptic. The philosophers who seemed to him to strengthen scepticism were, as he indicates in this manuscript, those like Fichte, Berkeley, and Kant, who tried to reconstruct philosophy upon metaphysical bases but failed to convince him of the validity of these bases. Hume, of course, made no such attempt; after reasoning his way into solipsism, he simply went on living, considering sceptical doubt of external reality to be a malady that he could never be entirely cured of, but that he could control by not dwelling too much in the mind.[23] Hume ends Part I of *A Treatise of Human Nature* by vowing not to be ruled by philosophy:

> Most fortunately it happens, that since reason is incapable of dispelling these clouds [questions and anxieties into which his philosophy has thrown him], nature herself suffices to that purpose, and cures me of this philosophical melancholy and delirium, either by relaxing this bent of mind, or by some avocation, and lively impression of my senses, which obliterate all these chimeras. I dine, I play a game of back-gammon, I converse, and am merry with my friends; and when after three or fours hours' amusement, I wou'd return to these speculations, they appear so cold, and strain'd, and ridiculous that I cannot find [it] in my heart to enter into them any farther.
>
> Here then I find myself absolutely and necessarily determin'd to live, and talk, and act like other people in the common affairs of life. (269)

Pater states in "The History of Philosophy," that Hume, with his scepticism "of the supposed inherent judgment of the understanding" cleared away metaphysical cobwebs and returned the mind to "the corrective experience of the senses." In the same manuscript he says that realizing the impossibility of proving metaphysical ideas or even of knowing "the mental substance of ourselves" can help one relax philosophically, or, more precisely, "bring us back with a great sense of relief after the long strain of a too curious self-inquiry to the phenomena of the superficial natural world."

Thus, the great Scottish philosopher could have set the example for Pater's turn toward sensuous appreciation in the second half of the "Conclusion." Pater could also have been familiar with the straightforward injunction of the sceptical Aristippus of Cyrene to appreciate the moment. Pater had had the opportunity, upon borrowing Zeller's *Die Philosophie der Griechen* from the Queen's College Library in December of 1863, to read a synopsis of the philosophy of Aristippus. He might have encountered it again in 1868. A review of Oswald J. Reichel's translation of Zeller's *Socrates and the Socratic Schools*, the part of *Die Philosophie der Griechen* including the section on Aristippus, appeared in the *Saturday Review of Politics, Science and Art* on 18 July, 1868 (93-5). This anonymous review either anticipates several of the ideas that were to become identified with Pater, or it was written by Pater himself.[24] However that may be, it is a matter of record that Pater had Zeller's book in his hands in 1863, and that Zeller gives a clear and complete summary of the philosophy of Aristippus, from the subjectivity of knowledge –

> Perceptions, being sensations of a change within ourselves, do not supply us with the least information as to things in themselves[25]

to the experiential ethic –

> The only rule of life is to cultivate the art of enjoying the present moment. The present only is ours. (356)

It is possible that Pater, not only when writing *Marius*, but also when writing the "Conclusion," considered the basic 'argument' in the "Conclusion" to be Cyrenaic.

There is a double irony in the idea that opens the second half of the "Conclusion": "The service of philosophy, and of religion and culture as well, to the human spirit, is to startle it into a sharp and eager observation." The first irony is that here philosophy is enlisted in an endeavour that seems antithetical to it – enriching observation without reflection; and the second is that the name of Novalis is associated with the endeavour. On the surface, Pater's idea, stated in the second sentence, seems just an explanation of the preceding statement, a quotation from Novalis: "To philosophize is to dephlegmatize – to vivify." But in Fragment No. 15 in the "Logologische Fragmente," from which the idea is taken, Novalis did not mean that philosophy should vivify by sharpening the eye.[26] Fichtean in orientation, he meant that it should vivify by creating awareness of the unifying principle of consciousness in oneself and in all living things. Pater simply disregarded the context of Novalis' statement and imposed his own; or perhaps when quoting he did not even remember the context.

It is very likely Ernest Renan who breathes beneath the misleading name of Novalis. Although Renan was not to appear in the library borrowings until 1883, when Pater borrowed *Mélanges d'histoire et de voyages*, he was referred to three times in "Coleridge's Writings" (111, 122, 131). The absence of borrowings of Renan's early works, coupled with Pater's demonstrated familiarity with some of them, suggests that Pater owned some of these works in the 1860s. The fact that five volumes of Renan's early works were in Pater's library at the time of his death[27] strengthens the likelihood. *Averroès et l'Averroïsme*, an early work by Renan that Pater was to paraphrase a passage from in "Pico della Miran-dola,"[28] is one that he was probably familiar with when he wrote "Coleridge's Writings" and the "Conclusion." This work could have helped Pater relate philosophy to spectacle, by maintaining that the history of philosophy was valuable as a spectacle. Renan develops this idea, as follows, in his Preface to *Averroès et l'Averroïsme*:

> from the moment when one admits that the history of the human soul is the greatest reality open to our investigations, all research to throw light on a corner of the past takes on a significance and a value. It is, in a sense, more important to know what the human spirit has thought on a problem than to have an opinion on that problem; for, even though the question is unsolvable, the work of the human spirit to solve it constitutes an experimental fact which always has its interest; and in supposing that philosophy should be condemned to always be only an eternal and vain effort to define the infinite, one cannot deny at least that there is in this effort, for curious spirits, a spectacle worthy of the highest attention.[29]

Pater had been very close to this humanistic, historicist statement of Renan's in "Winckelmann" when he had said: "Philosophy serves culture not by the fancied gift of absolute or transcendental knowledge, but by suggesting questions which help one to detect the passion and strangeness and dramatic contrasts of life."[30] Here, in the "Conclusion," he differs only in emphasizing concrete rather than abstract spectacles.

The emphasis in the middle sentences of the fifth paragraph on observation of concrete details suggests the experiential stance that Pater had attributed to Goethe in "Coleridge's Writings," when he stated: "The true illustration of the speculative temper is not the Hindoo, lost to sense, understanding, individuality; but such an one as Göthe, to whom every moment of life brought its share of experimental, individual knowledge, by whom no touch of the world of form, colour, and passion was disre-garded" (108). In this essay Pater also calls Goethe, as well as Renan "a true humanist," and one who "holds his theories lightly" (111). Like Hume and Renan, Goethe had helped to liberate Pater from the tyranny of philosophy.

Pater closes his fifth paragraph with a scientific image: "How may we pass most swiftly from point to point, to be present always at the focus where the greatest number of vital forces unite in their purest energy?" (311). The source of this image could be John Tyndall's "On the Relations of Radiant Heat to Chemical Constitution, Colour, Texture," the lead essay in the *Fortnightly Review* on 15 February, 1866. There is no proof that Pater read this article, but the least that can be claimed is that it is a scientific source that can explain the image. In his essay Tyndall reports several experiments conducted with flames. In one he presents to the imagination of the reader an experiment with lightless rays from an electric lamp. He collects these "dark rays" by means of a black liquid that separates them from the luminous rays. He states: "I bring these invisible rays to a focus at a distance of several feet from the electric lamp; the dark rays form there an invisible image of the source from which they issue. By proper means this invisible image may be transformed into one of dazzling brightness."[31] He emphasizes that at the focus where the rays converge there is no light and the air is "just as cold as the surrounding air," since the ether, the transmitting medium, is "detached from the air." He adds dramatically:

> But though you see it not, there is sufficient heat at that focus to set London on fire. The heat there at the present moment is competent to raise iron to a temperature at which it throws off brilliant scintillations. It can heat platinum to whiteness and almost fuse that refractory metal. It actually can fuse gold, silver, copper, and aluminium. The moment, moreover, that wood is placed at the focus it bursts into a blaze.(9-10)

Pater had used imagery strikingly like Tyndall's in "Winckelmann," composed just a few months after Tyndall's essay appeared, in writing an analogy to explain how Browning was able to take characters unremarkable in themselves (like the invisible dark rays, one may say) and put them into a situation that 'glorifies' them. He states: "To realize this situation, to define in a chill and empty atmosphere [like Tyndall's cold air, separate from the ether] the focus where rays, in themselves pale and impotent, unite and begin to burn, the artist has to employ the most cunning detail, to complicate and refine upon thought and passion a thousand-fold" (99-100, 214). It seems that Tyndall's invisible rays also inspired the image in the "Conclusion" of the focus where "vital forces unite in their purest energy."

The first sentence of the sixth paragraph presents the most famous image in Pater's works: "To burn always with this hard gem-like flame, to maintain this ecstasy, is success in life." In context, it seems that this flame is the same as that in the preceding sentence, the flame at the focus of the pale rays. But why does Pater call it gem-like? Which gem does he have in mind? Why does he call the flame hard? I think it possible that in his memory Pater had conflated two images of flame described in Tyndall's essay. At another point Tyndall describes the oxyhydrogen flame which, like the pure flame from the dark rays, would be invisible in a clean atmosphere. He says that its temperature is 6000 degrees Fahrenheit and that 2000 degrees is hot enough to fuse cast iron. He adds: "When this flame impinges on a piece of lime, we have the dazzling Drummond light"

(5-6). In other words, heating calcium oxide in the flame of an oxy-hydrogen torch produces calcium hydroxide; and, according to the *New Columbia Encyclopedia*, during this reaction "much heat is given off and the solid nearly doubles its volume" – and the dazzling, white Drummond light, or limelight, radiates forth.[32] Thus Tyndall calls to mind the brightest light known to nineteenth-century eyes, blazing from lime turned crystalline. If Pater had this light in mind when he wrote "a hard gem-like flame," the gem is a diamond – hard and radiant. This image relates the "ecstasy" of the "Conclusion," which seems the summum bonum of earthly life, to "the supreme moral charm of the Beatrice of the Commedia," referred to in "Diaphaneitè," of which Pater states: "It does not take the eye by breadth of colour; rather it is that fine edge of light, where the elements of our moral nature refine themselves to the burning point."[33] When this generalized refining fire, as well as the generalized "clear crystal nature" of Diaphaneitè (253), are remembered, it is easy to see why Pater would have been struck by Tyndall's heat and light images. The focus of the purest rays, the heat hot enough to fuse metals, and the dazzling diamond-like limelight gave him exactly the scientific, imagistic detail he could use to individualize his rather conventional general concepts. This imagery was to persist in his works. In "Dante Gabriel Rossetti," he says of Dante Alighieri: "To him, in the vehement and impassioned heat of his conceptions, the material and the spiritual are fused and blent: if the spiritual attains the definite visibility of a crystal, what is material loses its earthiness and impurity."[34] And in "The Genius of Plato," he states: "For him [Plato], as for Dante, in the impassioned glow of his conceptions, the material and the spiritual are blent and fused together. While, in that fire and heat, what is spiritual attains the definite visibility of a crystal, what is material, on the other hand, will lose its earthiness and impurity."[35] The gem-like flame, thus, is associated with white light, the perfect fusion of material and spiritual elements, and Dantean ecstasy.

The implication in the remainder of the sixth paragraph is that what passes for life is often death-in-life, or, to use Pater's image, sleeping before evening. Pater's dominant message is *Wake up and look*: "While all melts under our feet, we may well catch at any exquisite passion, or any contribution to knowledge that seems by a lifted horizon to set the spirit free for a moment, or any stirring of the senses, strange dyes, strange flowers and curious odours, or work of the artist's hands, or the face of one's friend" (311). Pater had long been familiar with the idea that art lifts one above the enslavement of the world. In the *Ästhetik*, Hegel discusses at length the power of poetry to create a sense of freedom. To Hegel art was superior to nature because it proceeded from creative mind, whereas nature was bound by laws of necessity. He states: "what we enjoy in artistic beauty is just the *freedom* of its creative and plastic activity. In the production and contemplation of these we appear to escape from the principle of rule and system" (I, 6). Art also, according to Hegel, gives one something to cling to in the flux: "The individual living thing ... is transitory; it vanishes and is unstable in its external aspect. The work of art persists" (I, 39). And it was probably Hegel who introduced Pater to the idea of the expanded moment, as it relates to painting. For Hegel it was painters who were to seek expansion of the moment, because painting can embody only one moment in time (III, 295). Pater had already extended the concept to poetry in a reference in "Winckelmann" to Browning's expanded moments. In the "Conclusion," he simply takes the concept a step further, extending the expanded moment to perceptions of the real world.

In spite of his indebtedness to Hegel, Pater is quite un-Hegelian in grouping impressions from life and art together, as he does, for example, in the phrases the "work of the artist's hands, or the face of one's friend." Hegel assumed that the perceiver and the perceived work of art were both autonomous: "He [the perceiver] suffers it [the art object] to exist in its free independence as an object" (I, 49). But Hegel did not assume that people could treat other people as if they were autonomous works of art. In "Diaphaneitè" Pater removed the distinction between life and art, recommending that people be treated "in the spirit of art," or, in other words, like autonomous works of art. And here, in the "Conclusion," he writes compellingly about observing and perceiving works of art, live hands and faces, hills – without making any distinction between what is expected from art objects, live objects, and natural scenery. This tendency to obliterate the distinction between life and art is the most startling element in the "Conclusion," because it makes life, like art, something, not to be participated in, but simply to be appreciated. To treat life in the spirit of art is to create stasis. It is true that there is one expression in the sixth paragraph of the "Conclusion" that seems to move the persona from the spectator's stance into participation. Pater states: "gathering all we are into one desperate effort to see and touch, we shall hardly have time to make theories about the things we see and touch." Touching, here, however, seems to be merely a mode of perception, as it was to Berkeley, who wrote extensively about seeing and touching, especially in *A New Theory of Vision*, Sections XLV-XLIX. For Berkeley, it was necessary to touch a tangible object in order to perceive it fully.

Near the end of the sixth paragraph Pater asserts the right to explore impressions and opinions eclectically, without allegiance to any system that would restrict vision or choice. In selecting Comte and Hegel as thinkers whose "facile orthodoxy" he will not submit to, he is divorcing himself from the two chief, opposing schools of philosophy at Oxford in his day, the positivist and the transcendental.[36] (Hegel's aesthetic philosophy is probably not at issue here.) He thus is claiming for himself the widest range of choice, in terms that his readers will understand. A surface reading of the next passage would suggest that Pater was indebted to Victor Hugo for the idea that philosophy is an instrument for enlarging and diversifying one's experience, since he quotes Hugo's statement from *Les Misérables* ("Jean Valjean," Bk. II, ch. 2) that "philosophy is the microscope of thought." But as in the case of Novalis, Pater sets the quotation from the source into a context that places a new interpretation upon it. In Hugo's context the statement has nothing to do with eclectic appreciation; it means that nothing can escape the upright moral eye of philosophy – no evil, equivocation, or falsehood. Beneath Pater's eclectic manifesto, as beneath the related quotation from Novalis, we find the presence of Renan. In "The Religions of Antiquity" (1857), which appears to have been Pater's principal source of ideas on religion in "Coleridge's Writings" and "Winckelmann," Renan states:

> Eclecticism is ... the obligatory method of our age. ... Schools are in science what parties are in politics: each one is right by turns; it is impossible for an enlightened man to shut himself up in one of them so exclusively as to shut his eyes to what the others hold to be reasonable.[37]

Thus, even in asserting eclectic independence, Pater likely was following a precursor, Renan.

The final paragraph of the "Conclusion" opens with Pater's mistaken reference to the sixth book of Rousseau's *Confessions*. Pater uses the reference to enhance the main thrust of the paragraph, his advocacy of intellectual excitement. Although in Book VI Rousseau describes, as Pater says, the onset of what he thought to be a "mortal disease," he does not, as Pater says, determine that the remainder of his time can best be spent "by intellectual excitement, which he found in the clear, fresh writings of Voltaire." As Gerald Monsman has pointed out, Voltaire is not mentioned in Book VI.[38] Also, Rousseau does not seek intellectual excitement, to expand the interval before death. He resolves to make the most of his time by employing his mind "in more noble cares, as anticipating those I should soon have to attend, and which I had till then much neglected."[39] His studious and religious reading lead to intellectual excitement, but have not been undertaken for it.

Pater next generalizes the idea of the interval before death by referring accurately to Victor Hugo's statement, "we are all condamnés," although he did not remember the exact source of the statement or did not want to clutter his text with it. As Marcel Françon has observed, the source is *Le Dernier Jour d'un condamné (The Last Day of the Condemned)*,[40] a story in which a prisoner condemned to death keeps a journal of his thoughts and feelings until almost the moment of his execution. At one point he consoles himself with the idea that all people are condemned to death, although some with an "indefinite reprieve."[41]

In concluding the "Conclusion" with a straightforward assertion that the best way to spend the interval before death is in intellectual excitement, or multiplied consciousness, and the best way to achieve this state is by the love of art for art's sake, Pater suggests the influence of Baudelaire, as well as that of Morris. There is no certain link between Pater and Baudelaire at this time; Pater does not mention Baudelaire by name until 1876, in "Romanticism." But it would have been difficult for the alert man of letters and reader of Swinburne that Pater was in 1867 and 1868 not to have been familiar with Baudelaire's works. In "Charles Baudelaire: *Les Fleurs du mal*," in the *Spectator*, on 6 September, 1862, Swinburne had associated Baudelaire with the idea that "the poet's business is ... to write good verses, and by no means to redeem the age and remould society" (998). In *William Blake* (1866) he had used the term *art for art's sake* in a passage in which he had also referred to Baudelaire as "a living critic of incomparably delicate insight and subtly good sense, him-self 'impeccable' as an artist."[42] On 1 January, 1868, his elegy on Baudelaire, "Ave atque Vale," appeared in the *Fortnightly Review*. Pater had been aware of Swinburne ever since he had caught a glimpse of him in the autumn of 1858 walking near Headington, and he owned copies of *Chastelard* and *Atalanta in Calydon*.[43] He probably learned the term *art for art's sake* and its association with Baudelaire from Swinburne.

From internal evidence it appears that the idea of "multiplied consciousness" came from Baudelaire's "Le Poème du haschische," in *Les Paradis artificiels*. Baudelaire explains in this work the rewards of drug-induced acuteness of consciousness:

> If you are one of these souls [the modern *homme sensible*], your innate love of form and color will initially find great pasturage in the earliest developments of your intoxication. Colors will assume unaccustomed strength, and will enter your mind with triumphant intensity. ... Craggy countrysides, receding horizons, city vistas whitened by the ghastly lividity of a storm, or lit by the dense heat of setting suns ... the first sentence that hits your eyes, if they should happen to fall upon a book; in short, everything – the whole univer-sality of existence – rises before you with a new and hitherto unsus-pected glory.[44]

Of course, Baudelaire does not recommend smoking hashish; he calls it "slow suicide." But he does regard the heightened state of mind as paradisical, an ultimate value. As one can see in the following passage, he condemns the means, not the end of intoxication:

> But man is not so forsaken, so deprived of any *honest* means of reaching heaven, that he should be obliged to turn to pharmacy and witchcraft; he need not sell his soul to pay for the intoxicating kisses and affection of the Houri. (81)

And what honest means does Baudelaire suggest? In a word, art. To epitomize the divine intoxication he pictures a man on "the lofty summit of Olympus"; "all about him the Muses of Raphael or Mantegna compose their sublimest dances to solace him for his long fastings and constant prayers. ... Divine Apollo, master of every art ... gently sets his bow to the most vibrant strings" (82). In contrast to the "false happiness" resorted to by the poor creatures of the earth who need drugs for excitement, he sets the true happiness of artists: "we, the poets and philosophers, have regenerated our souls through constant work and meditation; through the conscientious use of our Will, and the enduring loftiness of our Purpose,

we made ourselves a garden of true beauty" (82). Pater could have
borrowed from Baudelaire not only the idea that the artist holds an
advantage in the pursuit of multiplied consciousness, but also the idea that
passionate devotees of other ideals may achieve the state. In his famous
prose poem "Enivrez-vous," he advises: "Lest you be martyred slaves of
Time, intoxicate yourselves, be drunken without cease! With wine, with
poetry, with virtue, or with what you will."[45] This pronouncement finds its
parallel in Pater's statement that "High passions give one this quickened
sense of life, ecstasy and sorrow of love, political or religious enthusiasm,
or the 'enthusiasm of humanity.' Only, be sure it is passion."

And so, beneath the surface of Pater's text, the muses hum – Goethe,
Renan; Fichte, Hume; Spencer, Tyndall; Hegel, Aristippus, Plato; Morris, Baudelaire. I do not mean that Pater's "Conclusion" is a pastiche of
other writers' ideas, but that throughout an eight-year period, by selective
reading, Pater accumulated ideas to which he felt affinities, assimilated
them, and on a brilliant occasion expressed them in the "Conclusion." His
originality is in the unique synthesis and the compelling expression.

BILLIE ANDREW INMAN
University of Arizona

NOTES

1. "Poems by William Morris," *Westminster Rev.*, 90 (Oct. 1868), 309.
2. *The Earthly Paradise*, 3 vols. (London: Longmans, Green, 1900), I, 65.
3. *The Absent Father: Virginia Woolf and Walter Pater* (New Haven: Yale U.P., 1980),
   pp. 114, 115.
4. In a letter to John Chapman written 23 July, 1868, Pater refers to the review as being
   completed but not yet set in type (*Letters of Walter Pater*, ed. Lawrence Evans [Oxford:
   Clarendon Press, 1970], p. 5).
5. *Fortnightly Rev.*, 9 (1 April, 1 June, 1868), 353-73, 611-28; 10 (1 July, 1 Nov., 1868),
   61-80, 492-509.
6. *Fortnightly Rev.*, 10 (1 July, 1868), 16-40.
7. In 1851, Hugo von Mohl, in *Grundzüge der Anatomie und Physiologie der vegetabilis-
   chen Zelle* (Braunschweig: Friedrich Vieweg und Sohn, 1851), had discussed protoplasm and its association with cells; however, he had thought *Protoplasma* subordinate
   in older cells to what he called *Zellsaft* (cell sap), pp. 40-4, 44. This work was translated
   by Arthur Henfrey as *Principles of the Anatomy and Physiology of the Vegetable Cell*
   (London: John van Voorst, 1852).
8. Spencer was of course not the first to express these ideas. That distinction probably
   belongs to the leading researcher in the field of physiology in the first half of the
   nineteenth century, Johannes Peter Müller (1801-58), from 1835 a professor at the
   University of Berlin. His great work, *Handbuch der Physiologie des Menschens für
   Vorlesungen* was published between 1833 and 1840. A two-volume English translation
   of this work by William Baly, entitled *Elements of Physiology*, was published in London
   by Taylor and Walton, 1840-3. Although the verbal similarities between Spencer's and
   Pater's texts make Spencer seem Pater's source, Müller could conceivably have been
   the source. He succinctly explains two ideas voiced by Pater: that human beings are
   constituted of the same elements that exist in inorganic matter and in other organic
   matter, and that all organic compounds have a tendency to decompose (*Elements of
   Physiology*, trans. William Baly, arranged from the second London edition by John Bell

[Philadelphia: Lea and Blanchard, 1843], pp.13, 16). Pater could also have found in this book a list of fifteen elements that compose "man and the higher animals" (14).
9. *The Principles of Biology*, 2 vols. (New York: D. Appleton, 1897), I, 3-24, 50, 19.
10. Further information about all library borrowings referred to in this paper is given under the date of borrowing in my *Walter Pater's Reading: An Annotated Bibliography of His Library Borrowings and Literary References* (New York: Garland Publishing, 1981).
11. *The Philosophy of Fine Art*, trans. F.P.B. Osmaston, 4 vols. (London: G. Bell and Sons, 1920), I, 6.
12. *Westminster Rev.*, 85 (Jan. 1866), 109, 110.
13. *Fortnightly Rev.*, 12 (1 Nov., 1869), 501.
14. Permission to quote from Pater's unpublished manuscripts has been generously granted by Professor Sharon Bassett, California State University at Los Angeles, and Rodney G. Dennis, Curator of Manuscripts, the Houghton Library.
15. *The Vocation of Man*, trans. William Smith, in his *Popular Works of Johann Gottlieb Fichte*, 2 vols., 4th ed. (London: Trübner and Co., 1899), I, 327-8.
16. Alexander Bain had used the term *stream of consciousness* in "The Feelings and the Will, Viewed Physiologically," *Fortnightly Rev.*, 3 (15 Jan., 1866), 580. Whether Pater read this article is not known. If he did, he might have been influenced by the term; but he was not influenced by the context of the term, Bain's description of mental activity, which is quite different from Pater's in the "Conclusion."
17. *A Treatise of Human Nature*, ed. L.A. Selby-Bigge (Oxford: Clarendon Press, 1888), p.31.
18. *Physics*, trans. R.P. Hardie and R.K. Gaye, Bk. IV, ch.12, 220a, in *The Works of Aristotle*, Vol. I, *Great Books of the Western World* (Chicago: Encyclopædia Britannica, 1952), VIII, 300.
19. See *A New Theory of Vision*, XLV-XLIX, and *The Principles of Human Knowledge*, Part I, I-II.
20. I have discussed Pater's borrowing of Lewis Campbell's edition of *The Theætetus of Plato*, a revised text, with English notes (Oxford: Clarendon Press, 1861), in *Walter Pater's Reading*, under 10 March–26 March, 1863.
21. *The Dialogues of Plato*, trans. Benjamin Jowett, *Great Books of the Western World* (Chicago: Encyclopædia Britannica, 1952), VII, 520.
22. He states in *Marius the Epicurean*, for example: "in the reception of metaphysical *formulæ*, all depends, as regards their actual and ulterior result, on the pre-existent qualities of that soil of human nature into which they fall" (Library Ed., 2 vols. [London: Macmillan, 1910], I, 135-6); and he refers to "the opposite issues deducible from the same text" (I, 201).
23. *A Treatise of Human Nature*, p.218.
24. I argue in *Walter Pater's Reading*, under 18 July, 1868, that this review was written by Pater.
25. Eduard Zeller, *Socrates and the Socratic Schools*, trans. Oswald J. Reichel (London: Longmans, 1885; first published 1868), pp.348-9.
26. In *Neue Fragmentensammlungen* (1798), *Novalis Schriften*, 4 vols., ed. Paul Kluckhohn with Richard Samuel (Leipzig: Bibliographisches Institut, 1929), II, 321.
27. In a letter to me dated 27 May, 1977, Samuel Wright states that about 1965 he saw five volumes by Renan in the Pater collection at Miss Ottley's and that he made a note stating that they were published about 1860. It is reasonable to assume that one of these volumes was *Averroès et l'Averroïsme* (1861).
28. In *The Renaissance*, Library Ed., p.36. The title of the source is not given on the page, but the passage paraphrased can be found in *Averroès et l'Averroïsme, Œuvres complètes de Ernest Renan*, 10 vols. ed. Henriette Psichari (Paris: Calmann-Levy, 1947), III, 293.
29. *Œuvres complètes*, III, 18. Translation by Laura L. Inman.
30. "Winckelmann," *Westminster Rev..*, 87 (Jan. 1867), 109; in *The Renaissance*, Library Ed., p.230.
31. *Fortnightly Rev.*, 4 (15 Feb., 1866), 9.
32. Ed. William H. Harris and Judith S. Levey (New York: Columbia U.P., 1975), p.420,

s.v. *Calcium oxide*.
33. *Miscellaneous Studies*, Library Ed., pp. 247-8.
34. *Appreciations*, Library Ed., p. 212.
35. *Plato and Platonism*, Library Ed., p. 135.
36. Anonymous, "Study and Opinion in Oxford," *Macmillan's Magazine*, 21 (Dec. 1869), 184-92.
37. "The Religions of Antiquity," in *Studies of Religious History*, trans. Henry F. Gibbons (London: William Heinemann, 1893), p. 35.
38. *Walter Pater* (Boston: Twayne Publishers, 1977), p. 62.
39. *The Confessions of Jean-Jacques Rousseau*, anon. trans. of 1738 and 1790, rev. and completed A. S. B. Glover (New York: Heritage Press, 1955), p. 206.
40. "Pascal et Rousseau chez Walter Pater," *Romance Notes*, 14 (1973), 514-6.
41. The context is as follows:

> Condamné à mort!
> Eh bien, pourquoi non? *Les hommes*, je me rappelle l'avoir lu dans je ne sais quel livre où il n'y avait que cela de bon, *les hommes sont tous condamnés à mort avec des sursis indéfinis*. Qu'y a-t-il donc de si changé à ma situation? (*Œuvres complètes*, New ed. [Paris: Alexandre Houssiaux, 1863], IX, 323).

A volume of Victor Hugo's short novels including *Le Dernier Jour d'un condamné* was found in Pater's library at his death. The volume bears the title of one of the other novels: *Bug-Jargal* (Paris: Librairie de L. Hachette, 1863). This volume is now in the possession of John Sparrow.
42. *William Blake: A Critical Essay*. New ed. (New York: E. P. Dutton, 1906), p. 100.
43. The source of the reference to Pater's first glimpse of Swinburne is a letter from John Rainier McQueen to Thomas Wright, 26 March, 1904, in the Wright Manuscript Correspondence at the Lilly Library, Indiana University. Copies of *Chastelard: A Tragedy* and *Atalanta in Calydon*, both published in London by Edward Moxon in 1865, were found in Pater's personal library at his death, both signed *Walter H. Pater*, in the vertical hand of the 1860s and the early 1870s. They are now in the collection of John Sparrow.
44. *The Artificial Paradise*, trans. Ellen Fox (New York: Herder and Herder, 1971), pp. 67-9.
45. Trans. Guy Thorne, in *Charles Baudelaire* (New York: Brentano's, 1915), p. 127.

Pater's Criticism: Some Distinctions

During the course of the past decade it has become increasingly possible to categorize the general methods that literary historians have used in order to explore Pater's critical writing; in addition it has become possible to see those categories corresponding to three methodological practices. All of these practices have depended fundamentally upon a simple historicism. The first (and, methodologically, the simplest) involves considering Pater's critical work in terms of his commerce with the influence, principles and achievement of some important contemporary figures: Jowett, Arnold, Ruskin, Newman and so on. The second line of investigation employs a similar but rather more sophisticated methodology: it involves placing his essays and the critical statements or assumptions that they embody against a specific tradition of nineteenth-century criticism on the same topics. Consequently, it is claimed, it becomes possible to assess Pater's accounts of (say) Marcus Aurelius Antoninus or Leonardo or Plato in terms of his orthodoxy or originality. The third 'group' (although in practice it barely amounts to such a description) is historicist in the sense that it is concerned with what it sees as the 'modernism' inherent in Pater's criticism. It sees Pater as a precursor of 'modern' critics, projecting or 'inscribing' upon a text or picture his own subjectivity.[1]

There is one major objection to the historicist methodology that these three methods of investigation employ. It has much in common with some recent objections to the simple historicism of post-war literary history.[2] The objection is to the allegedly self-evident nature of the disciplines of knowledge that literary historians have studied, and in particular it concerns the presupposition that criticism and the principles of aesthetic judgement that inform and confirm it belong to an autonomous, well-defined and so self-justifying discipline of knowledge: so that, for example, to describe the work of (to take an absurdly incongruous case) John Ruskin and Roland Barthes as *criticism* is to assume that their work can be meaningfully compared, to presuppose that they are in some way doing the same 'thing.' But the general movements and fashions of (what I shall, for the sake of expedience, have to call) literary and art criticism suggest that indeed they might not be the same 'thing' insofar as they invoke vastly different models of man to validate both their domain of knowledge and their discursive practices.[3] So, for example, post-Saussurean structuralist criticism depends in the first place upon a linguistic model of human activity – upon the concept of man as a sign-making animal – to validate it.

Marxist criticism, in its turn, depends upon what Foucault has called[4] an "economic" model of human activity for its validation. Now it is abundantly clear that the epistemological assumptions that made nineteenth-century criticism possible have received scant attention from historians and Pater's work has naturally suffered from this general neglect. The object of this essay, then, is to examine some of Pater's more famous critical utterances in order to isolate what *types* of critical statement they constitute; and then to argue that these *types* of statement answer to different *types* of arguments about art and aesthetic value which in their turn answer to radically opposed models of man.

One type of critical statement that I have in mind is made, in different essays, with regard to Michelangelo. The first occurrence is in a famous passage from the essay on Luca Della Robbia in *The Renaissance*:

> [T]his effect Michelangelo gains by leaving nearly all his sculpture in a puzzling sort of incompleteness, which suggests rather than realises actual form. Something of the wasting of that snow-image which he moulded at the command of Piero de' Medici, when the snow lay one night in the court of the *Pitti* palace, almost always lurks about it, as if he had determined to make the quality of a task, exacted from him half in derision, the pride of all his work. Many have wondered at that incompleteness, suspecting, however, that Michelangelo himself loved and was loath to change it, and feeling at the same time that they too would lose something if the half-realised form ever quite emerged from the stone, so rough-hewn here, so delicately finished there; and they have wished to fathom the charm of this incompleteness.[5]

As Pater's editor notes, the argument is reiterated in the essay "The Poetry of Michelangelo":

> As I have already pointed out, he secures that ideality of expression which in Greek sculpture depends on a delicate system of abstraction, and in early Italian sculpture on lowness of relief, by an incompleteness, which is surely not always undesigned, and which, as I think, no one regrets, and trusts to the spectator to complete the half-emergent form.   (*Hill*, 59, 25-32)

Several questions are suggested by these passages. The most important for my argument concerns the meaning of Pater's term "incomplete." What does it mean to say that a work of art is, or can be, "incomplete"? What is clearly *not* in Pater's mind is simply the notion of "wanting some part, unfinished, imperfect, defective" (OED) which would be appropriate to a description of (say) *Edwin Drood*. If the incompleteness of Michelangelo's work is "not always undesigned" there can be no sense in which the work is unfinished. (Neither, if the work is to be, as Pater claims, expressive, can it possibly be unfinished without jeopardising that very quality of expressiveness.) The quality of incompleteness that Pater is claiming for Michelangelo's work is not a defect in the art-object, but a constituent feature of it in the sense that it allows the individual spectator partly to construct his own experience of that art-object. Or to use the precise formulation of Roman Ingarden, which elucidates perfectly Pater's case, and to which I shall return later, the *lacunae* in the art-object (for Pater, its "incompleteness"; for Ingarden its "areas of indeterminateness") allow for the constitution of the aesthetic object.[6] I will pick up later some of the implications of this sort of observation, but for the moment it is sufficient to notice that the type of statement that Pater is making will depend ultimately (as it does with Roman Ingarden) upon a theory of perception and so upon a psychology of personality.

The difference between statements of this sort and other types of statement to be found in Pater's work is quite arresting. In *The Renaissance* Pater alludes (admittedly with some qualifications) to the *produced* nature of works of art. The claim that art-works were, among other things, products, was an increasingly popular idea in the nineteenth century. To the best of my knowledge, it is first made systematically by Auguste Comte;[7] it is a concern central to nineteenth-century Marxism and to late nineteenth-century English socialists like William Morris. The implications of it are far-reaching.

If literary and art works are products, then how they are marked off as art, the constraints upon their production, the manner in which they are consumed – these issues become a major topic for the critic to investigate as well as – for example – the formal features of the art-object. Moreover, if the art-object with which the critic is concerned is described as a product answering, like all other human products, to man's needs, then the production and consumption of that object is best explored in terms of the institution to which the art-object belongs. And this institutional account of art describes the relationships that exist between producer, product and consumer. Insofar as the art-object performs a function within this institution, so inevitably it can be appropriated to and explained by the discourses of history and economics.

Pater's first reference to how literary art-works are distinguished from other historically determined forms of discourse is made in "Two Early French Stories" in *The Renaissance*:

> For the student of manners, and of the old French language and literature, it has much interest of a purely antiquarian order. To say of an ancient literary composition that it has an antiquarian interest, often means that it has no distinct æsthetic interest for the reader of to-day. Antiquarianism, by a purely historical effort, by putting its object in perspective, and setting the reader in a certain point of view, from which what gave pleasure to the past is pleasurable for him also, may often add greatly to the charm we receive from ancient literature. But the first condition of such aid must be a real, direct, æsthetic charm in the thing itself. Unless it has that charm, unless some purely artistic quality went to its original making, no

merely antiquarian effort can ever give it an æsthetic value, or make
it a proper subject of æsthetic criticism. This quality, wherever it
exists, it is always pleasant to define, and discriminate from the sort
of borrowed interest which an old play, or an old story, may very
likely acquire through a true antiquarianism.

(*Hill*, 14,25——15,12)

This is a very confusing passage, not least because Pater runs together the
evaluative and definitional meanings of the terms "artistic" and "aesthetic." (Is, for example, the phrase "aesthetic charm" evaluative or descrip-
tive?) But in the distinction between the antiquarian and the aesthetic
Pater appears to be proposing a simple distinction between ordinary
discourses existing in a social and historical context and those that are
marked off as art-objects. Pater alleges that literary art is distinguished
ontologically by the existence of some formal property or properties that
are transhistorical in nature. The definition of that formal property
("aesthetic charm") is never supplied, but in Pater's mind it is related to
the expressiveness of the work ("the artistic quality [that] went into its
original making"). This quality seems to guarantee the privileged status of
the art-object: in the "Style" essay and *Plato and Platonism* Pater emphasizes that expressiveness is the defining feature of literary art:

> The one word for the one thing, the one thought, amid the
> multitude of words, terms, that might just do: the problem of style
> was there! – the unique word, phrase, sentence, paragraph, essay, or
> song, absolutely proper to the single mental presentation or vision
> within. In that perfect justice, over and above the many contingent
> and removable beauties with which beautiful style may charm us,
> but which it can exist without, independent of them yet dexterously
> availing itself of them, omnipresent in good work, in function at
> every point, from single epithets to the rhythm of a whole book, lay
> the specific, indispensable, very intellectual, beauty of literature,
> the *possibility of which constitutes it a fine art.*[8]

Immediately, however, the arguments of the works I have cited run into
three problems which are never resolved. First: Pater claims in "Two
Early French Stories" that a formal quality ("aesthetic charm") is a
necessary and sufficient condition for an object to be a work of art. It is in
fact insufficient. In *Plato and Platonism* craftsmanship and ways of life are
all characterised by the title "art." Second: expressiveness, which Pater
claims in the passage from the "Style" essay quoted above as constituting
literary art, is generally held to be a feature of the biography of the artist
and not a feature of the art-object (considered solely as an art-object). It
is moreover a quality that can be predicated of any artifact. What marks
off expressive art from expressive artifacts is a problem that is often
broached but never addressed in Pater's work. Third, and most importantly, it is difficult to conceive of expressiveness occurring outside of
institutional conventions: in the case of literature, outside that part of the

institution constituted by the reader or readers, for these determine the extent, if not the nature, of a work's expressiveness. Expressiveness, that is, the existence of which had seemed for Pater to offer the possibility of distinguishing art-objects from other objects, is itself only possible if art-objects are said to be in the first place socially or institutionally produced. (And if this is so it follows that their production can therefore be investigated in the same way as that of other products.) The question of the institution of art – the audience or reader for example – as the determinant of the expressiveness of art occurs uneasily in the last sentences of the "Style" essay where Pater begrudgingly acknowledges the social element of art: that the nature of its social functions sets off – in the words of that essay – "great" from "good" art.

The problem for Pater, then, both practically and theoretically, was how to accommodate the concept of an aesthetic object with the notion that art has a produced element to it. My own surmise is that Pater's failure to achieve a successful synthesis of these two positions had nothing to do with the compatibility or incompatibility of the theories in themselves, but with the tensions between the opposing models of human activity from which (for the nineteenth-century mind) they derived their validation. Now it is clear from Pater's concern in *The Renaissance* with "the fairer forms of nature and human life" (*Hill*, xx, 18-19) that the aesthetic experience which he envisaged was of a sort that did not *necessarily* involve the experience of art: art was generally important for it, but it was not a necessary precondition. It was an experience deriving from an attitude that could engage any naturally occurring phenomenon or object, and if the concern of Pater's aesthetic critic was principally an affective state in the mind of the perceiver, then this was a logical and perfectly admissible position to take.[9] (Pater, interestingly, ran together the following ontologically distinct *classes* of objects in *The Renaissance*: "the picture, the landscape, the engaging personality in life or in a book, *La Gioconda*, the hills of Carrara, Pico of Mirandola" (*Hill*, xx, 23-5): they can all give rise to what can legitimately be called an aesthetic object.) However, the sort of critical statement that talks of the produced nature of art *must* take as its subject art-objects or artifacts and the social conditions that accord them their privileged status. The first point that arises from this observation is that the two sorts of critical statements to be found in Pater's criticism do not necessarily agree upon what they can legitimately discuss. One limits its concern to aesthetic states and the other to art-objects and what produces them. This really leads to a second and more profound point.

One of the major theoretical issues in late nineteenth-century criticism – and so in Pater's work – was that theories of art were confronting – perhaps for the first time in the history of British art – theories of aesthetic experience, and each particular theory marked out for itself a different frame of reference. Perhaps the most detailed attempt to maintain that the theory of art and the theory of aesthetic experience are really quite separate has been made by the Polish philosopher, Roman Ingarden.

Whether or not these views are finally defensible is not my primary interest. What *is* central is the way Ingarden's categories clarify and illuminate at a theoretical level the relationship between the two types of critical statement that I have claimed are to be found in Pater's work.

Ingarden maintained that artistic value – if it exists – is something that arises in a work of art itself and has existential ground in that alone.[10] Aesthetic value, on the other hand, is something that manifests itself in the aesthetic, and not the artistic, object. For Ingarden what characterises art are its *lacunae*, its areas of indeterminateness. For the constitution of the aesthetic object these *lacunae* have to be made concrete, and so what he calls the "co-creative" activity of the observer is necessary. If this is the case then it follows that several, if not many, aesthetic objects may emerge on the basis of one work of art, and quite legitimately so, without recourse to the notion of a changed art-object as the justification for their separate existences. Ingarden claims that the aesthetic can be said to be definitive of a special mode of perception and so be considered as self-contained and independent of everything outside the perceiver. Thus the kinds of quality appropriate to it are intrinsic to the mode itself, or – and this is more likely – to the relationship between the work and the audience or spectator or reader. Hence, Ingarden adds, there is a special category of aesthetic terms that are used to describe the aesthetic object rather than stylistic or formal features of the art-object: Ingarden cites terms like "affected" or "artificial" (Pater uses terms like "strange," "exquisite" and so on).

Ingarden goes on to demonstrate that "art" is a far broader concept, and criticism of the art-object may include many considerations other than aesthetic perception. The tradition within which a work arises; the skill and intention of the artist; the social, psychological, political, and economic conditions out of which the work is produced: these are perhaps the most important of these considerations. So, putting Ingarden's theory simply, appreciation of art is more than aesthetic appreciation; and neither, it should be noted, do their fields of application of *necessity* overlap. In Ingarden's theory aesthetic value can derive from objects or experiences that one cannot describe in terms of art: sunsets (or landscapes or patterns of snow or any naturally occurring object) can become the legitimate basis for an aesthetic experience, but they don't as a consequence become works of art (or, in Oscar Wilde's phrase, "second-rate Turners"). Of course (Ingarden adds) no one would care to deny that there is a large measure of overlapping; in other words, that most aesthetic objects are clearly derived from art-objects.

Now the objections that can be raised to Ingarden's theory – and there are a great many – are not really relevant for my purposes, for it is clear that some of the problems in Pater's criticism, as well as some of the contradictions and conflicts in late nineteenth-century criticism generally, can be illuminated by adducing it as an explanation. Pater's programme for aesthetic or impressionist criticism, with its emphasis upon the critic's exclusive concern for his experience of the picture or the text, inevitably depends upon arguments broadly in line with what Ingarden proposes (although in the nature of things, these arguments were never stated so explicitly). Pater's "impressionist" critical theory attempts to describe the conditions under which the creation of the aesthetic object becomes possible: it had to do so by adducing a theory of perception and a psychology of personality to validate its procedures (in much the same way as modern structuralist critics adduce a linguistic model in order to propose a broadly similar view of aesthetic experience). These, in their turn, derived from a biological model; that is to say, from the hypothesis that man is an organism receiving stimuli and reacting to them.[11] Other explanations of human behaviour – like those models that seek to account for corporate or collective human activity or human actions that are not related to stimulus-reception – simply could not be accommodated into this biological model.[12] And, because in a nineteenth-century biological model human activity is constituted by a series of functional responses, contemporary accounts of aesthetic response validated by it had necessarily to fail to account for art as a social phenomenon: they had, that is, to fail to affiliate the concept of aesthetic response to the concept of art. Descriptions of art as a social phenomenon drew upon a contradictory explanation of human activity, one underwritten by the discourse of economics in which human activity is defined as a series of needs or desires that are answered or provided for by a series of products. And so such descriptions could set about explaining the origin of the class of objects marked off as art-objects and then the possibility of a culturally shared or common reaction to them. The tension between the two positions is one, as I have said, that is never resolved in Pater's critical practice, and one that helps give it its peculiarly evasive, provisional quality.

IAN SMALL
University of Birmingham

NOTES

1. Typical examples of the first kind are: Wendell Harris, "Arnold, Pater, Wilde and the Object as in Themselves They See It," *Studies In English Literature*, 11 (1971), 733-47; Gerald Monsman, "Pater, Hopkins and the Self," *Victorian Newsletter*, 46 (1974), 1-5.

   The methodology of the second group that I have in mind was perhaps first employed in Louise M. Rosenblatt, "The Genesis of *Marius The Epicurean*," *Comparative Literature*, 14 (1962), 242-60; it was one that I used in "Plato and Pater: Fin-de-Siècle Aesthetics," *British Journal of Aesthetics*, 12 (1972), 369-83; a more recent use is in Barrie Bullen, "Walter Pater's *Renaissance* and Leonard da Vinci's Reputation in the Nineteenth Century," *Modern Language Review*, 74 (1979), 268-80.

   It is a commonplace to talk of the 'modernity' of Pater's *oeuvre*; but only recently has this description been extended to his critical work. The best example of my third category is perhaps in Gerald Monsman, *Walter Pater's Art of Autobiography* (London: Yale U.P., 1980), pp. 9-36.

2. I am thinking both of the explicit rejection of periodicity in, for example, David Lodge, "Historicism and Literary History: Mapping the Modern Period," *New Literary History*, 10 (1979), 547-54 and the redefinition of the concept of literary history made in

Hans Robert Jauss, "Literary History as a Challenge to Literary Theory," *New Literary History*, 2 (1970), 7-37.

3. This kind of observation has been made most cogently with regard to the changes in the way the term "art" has been understood. See Paul Oskar Kristeller, "The Modern System of the Arts," *Journal of the History of Ideas*, 12 (1951), 496-527 and 13 (1952), 17-46. Kristeller doesn't discuss the history of post-Kantian aesthetics.

4. See Michel Foucault, *The Order of Things* (London: Tavistock, 1970), pp. 355-67 and *The Archeology of Knowledge* (London: Tavistock, 1972), passim.

5. Walter Pater, *The Renaissance*, ed. Donald Hill (London: U. of California Press, 1980), p. 53, 5-20. Hereafter all quotations from this work will be annotated in the text as *Hill* followed by page and line numbers.

6. See Roman Ingarden, "Artistic and Aesthetic Values," in *Aesthetics*, ed. Harold Osborne (Oxford: Oxford U.P., 1978), pp. 39-54. It is probably helpful to emphasise here that the "aesthetic object" is for Ingarden a purely mental, and *not* a physical, object.

7. See, for example, Auguste Comte, *A General View of Positivism*, trans. J. H. Bridges, 2nd ed. (London: Reeves and Turner, 1880), pp. 202-35.

8. Walter Pater, *Appreciations* (London: Macmillan, 1910), pp. 29-30 (my italics).

9. One can see implicit in this line of argument the justification for much of the criticism of Aestheticism in the 1880s, particularly that of George Du Maurier in his cartoons for *Punch*. Du Maurier's Aesthetes can manufacture from the most trivial artifact an excessive or extravagant aesthetic response. The most pointed of Du Maurier's cartoons appeared between the years 1879 and 1881.

10. Ingarden, pp. 39-42.

11. Pater's eclectic attitude to science and his dependence upon scientific sources is fairly well known – see *Hill*, pp. 452-4 for examples. My argument does not really limit itself to this sort of observation, but is much more concerned with the predominance of the models of human activity that informed the sciences themselves. I tried to broach the topic in "The Vocabulary of Pater's Criticism and the Psychology of Aesthetics," *British Journal of Aesthetics*, 18 (1978), 81-7. For the relationship between biology and psychology, see, for example, *Brett's History Of Psychology*, ed. R. S. Peters (London: George Allen and Unwin, 1953) and, more recently, D. B. Klein, *A Scientific History of Psychology* (London: Routledge and Kegan Paul, 1970).

12. This is not to deny that attempts were made to understand social action in terms of biology – particularly by Herbert Spencer. It is significant for my general case that these attempts were noticeably unsuccessful when they broached the topic of aesthetic response.

My thanks to Dr Charles Whitworth for his help with this essay.

Judas and the Widow

Thomas Wright and A. C. Benson as Biographers of Walter Pater: The Widow*

Walter Pater's death in July, 1894 took place towards the end of a century in which biography had great commercial success, and became one of the dominant literary modes. Accompanying its success was a protracted public debate about the nature of biography that revived on the publication of Froude's *Life of Carlyle* (which appeared between 1882 and 1884). Lytton Strachey's *Eminent Victorians* (1918) and *Queen Victoria* (1921) ended this phase of the debate resoundingly. Throughout the period two monuments of biography were built: the *Dictionary of National Biography* between 1886 and 1912, edited by Leslie Stephen and Sidney Lee, and Macmillan's English Men of Letters series, edited by John Morley, between 1878 and 1919.

Ultimately I wish to consider the problems raised by both of the principal early biographies of Walter Pater, by A. C. Benson (1862-1925; child of the Archbishop of Canterbury; Master at Eton 1885-1903; Fellow of Magdalene College, Cambridge, 1904-15, then Master of Magdalene) and Thomas Wright (1859-1936; school master, of the Cowper School, Olney), in the context of the debate, in particular what Edmund Gosse called in "The Ethics of Biography" "the duty of the biographer to the two hostile interests of the public and the family."[1] In an earlier article in 1901, "The Custom of Biography" Gosse had called for skilled professional authors, and characterised the worst of the untrained as "the Widow" biographers:

> This may be taken as a generic term for the class of life-writers whose only claim is that they are 'on the spot,' [commissioned] that arrogate to themselves the duty of biography merely because they are in possession of the documents. ... Her object is to present to the world an image of the deceased, which shall be deliberately although unconsciously false. ... She desires to show that he was perfect ... Above all, she carefully suppresses all evidence of his being unlike other men. ... For, it must be remarked, the Widow does not always boldly appear on the title-page: she often lurks behind the apparently unprejudiced name of some docile author. Her function, however, always is to stultify and misrepresent the life and character of the deceased; and the more devotion she thinks she is paying to his memory, the more completely she carries this out.[2]

*This is the first section of a longer piece on Benson and Thomas Wright as biographers of Pater.

Gosse presents his type flamboyantly, with overstatement, but with interesting modifications it describes Benson, who wrote with the co-operation and possibly the sponsorship of Pater's friends and relations; his relatively slim life of Pater appeared in the English Men of Letters series in 1906. Thomas Wright saw himself as an investigatory biographer, in both his life of Charles Dickens which was published in 1935 but written between 1900 and 1904, and in his two-volume life of Pater which appeared in 1907. For the Dickens life he found and documented the Ellen Ternan connection for the first time publicly, and in the Pater volumes Richard Jackson and J. R. McQueen. The *Daily Mail* reviewer of the Pater volumes commented wryly on Wright's tendency to uncover energetically the unexpected and Benson's contrastingly easeful devotion:

> After Mr. Benson, who strolled along alone to drop a rose on Pater's grave, comes Mr. Wright in his motor-omnibus, which he has crammed with extraordinary beings of whom none ever heard before, persons who, it appears, were intimately known to Pater.[3]

By many of his readers, particularly the interested ones – the Dickensians pre-eminently, but also the Pater circles – he was regarded as "Judas," to quote Oscar Wilde's description of the indiscreet biographer: "it is usually Judas who writes the biography."[4]

Very soon after Pater's death, within months, the affair and trials of Oscar Wilde commenced; sexual nonconformity became an open scandal, and was socially condemned. Also in 1895 appeared Edmund Purcell's *Life of Cardinal Manning*, which revealed Manning's suppressed early marriage, his despotic temper, his love of power, and his attacks on Newman, and this was followed by T. H. Henley's revelatory *Life of Burns* in 1897. These Lives occasioned vigorous public debate on questions of religious and sexual impropriety, and the discretion of biography. Purcell saw his *Life of Manning* as a test-case in an article in the *Nineteenth Century* in 1896:

> The question has been taken up on both sides of the Atlantic: Is it a virtue to suppress historic truth or no? The broad issues once raised cannot now be evaded. The advocates of the art of suppression in great histories or biographies, of historical facts, or of documents on which such facts are based, are now trembling in their shoes. They cannot lay the Frankenstein's monster they have raised.
>
> By force of circumstances, by its candour and outspokenness, and, perhaps, still more by the blunderings of its Catholic critics, the *Life of Cardinal Manning* is become a test-book, as it were: a criterion of the rival methods in the art of writing history or biography. In all the lands where the English tongue is spoken, the question of the hour is asked: Is the publication of historical facts based on authentic documents 'almost a crime' or a virtue?[5]

An anonymous critic writing in the *Academy* in 1901 on "Concerning

Biography" defends suppression, and hints at the sensationalism of the new biography by regretting "the journalising of a literary art." He looks backward for models and advocates discretion in a topical illustration:

> From Dr. Johnson's *Lives of the Poets* the biographer may learn the dignity of his art, and the enduring value of a reverent and sagacious handling of delicate subjects: as for instance where, in discussing Dryden's suspiciously timely conversion to Roman Catholicism, he puts the matter by.[6]

This critic refers approvingly to Gosse's "The custom of Biography" which had just appeared, and in which Gosse had contented himself with describing the English tradition of biography and attacking devotional overlong Lives: "We in England bury our dead under the monstrous catafalque of two volumes (crown octavo)."[7]

The *Academy* writer voices criticisms of the genre which underlie Gosse's 1901 comments and those of many others in literary periodicals of the day.

> The truth is, that of the biographies published, nearly all are written too soon, many ought not to be written at all, and the majority of the remainder could be of value only if they were half as long and twice as well done. ... And who, nowadays, would not be glad if biographies were many and small and good? It is the insatiate curiosity of the age which will neither wait patiently nor taste nicely.[8]

These complaints about size are specifically related by Gosse to the desirable compactness of the English Men of Letters biographies. By 1903 in "The Ethics of Biography" Gosse was more extreme: he did not content himself with attacking "devotional" and lengthy Lives but openly defended indiscretion in biography:

> Certain fashionable biographies of the present day deserve no other comment than the words 'A Lie' printed in bold letters across their title pages.[9]

It is "more and more difficult to learn the truth about an eminent person, if that truth can be considered in any sense undignified," he complains.[10] Consequently, he argues that the biographer's "anxiety should be, not how to avoid all indiscretion, but how to be as indiscreet as possible within the boundaries of good taste and kind feeling."[11] Where these boundaries lay was still being assessed in 1918 and later, when Lytton Strachey attempted to obliterate the enclosures entirely in *Eminent Victorians* and his life of Queen Victoria. I shall show how Benson, Gosse, and another critic, Robert Ross, differently adjudge the matter in the event of the Pater biography, but the degree of interest in the question at the time is indicated by its inclusion in two contrasting reviews of Benson's EML biography of Rossetti which appeared in 1904. The anonymous critic in the *Spectator* calls Benson "a new biographer of exceptional gifts of sympathy and judgement," but he does audibly regret and ponder the absence of an element of Rossetti's personality:

> The only side of Rossetti's nature at which Mr Benson does not even hint is his scornful yet Rabelaisian humour. ... Echoes of certain rhymed irreverences, caustic and vigorous float through our mind as we write these words; but whether there was any call for Mr. Benson to record them in a book in this series is a question which he has perhaps answered rightly by silence. And yet one or two, among the prose passages from the letters at the end, might had [sic] added another lamp with which to light this curious character.[12]

The *Athenaeum* reviewer is less favourably impressed by Benson's biography: "A good superficial view of the subject is conveyed; but the reader knows no more of the man as he lays down the book than he did as he opened it." He too objects, though more strongly than the author in the *Spectator*, to Benson's handling of these boundaries:

> As regards the most tragic episode of Rossetti's life, and that which may be supposed to have clouded its close, the information supplied is inadequate and in a sense misleading. There are two manners in which that painful subject, exact knowledge concerning which is in a few hands, may be treated. The truth may be told, or the subject may be, as it has hitherto been, ignored. What is said, however, on p. 49 as to speculation regarding the state of mind of the victim being 'worse than useless,' is itself 'worse than useless,' there being no room for speculation to arise.[13]

This reviewer goes on to consider Benson's treatment of two other delicate matters – Rossetti's "violation of the secrecy of the grave" and the poet's "indulgence in chloral hydrate." The intensity of the interest in this matter of what is included and how, and what suppressed, is unmistakable.

The use of letters figures importantly in this notion of "indiscretion" or honesty. William Mason's memoir and letters of Gray (1775) is an early example of the modern use of letters in biography. Purcell printed very revealing correspondence between Manning and Newman, and the ethics of the use of private letters and papers is often discussed. Gosse demands that the biographer "open letters" and "unclasp diaries." Leslie Stephen declares

> The question of whether a really satisfactory life can be written is essentially the question of whether letters have been preserved. ... It should therefore be regarded as a duty ... to keep all letters written by a possible biographee.[14]

Purcell, Gosse, and Stephen all manifest a consciousness of the method of biography and exude a desire for rigour and professionalism, but Stephen believes accuracy primarily to lie in the former intimacy of the biographer with his subject, and Gosse in the professionalism and skill of the biographer. Where Stephen writes in 1893

> Nothing is more striking to the biographer than the rapidity with which all possibility of satisfactory portraiture vanishes. Nobody, as Johnson somewhere says, could write a satisfactory life of a man who had not lived in habits of intimacy with him.[15]

Gosse implies in 1901 that he would prefer a professional who never knew the biographee to an inexpert interested "Widow." By 1894, then, and in the decade following Pater's death, the nature of biography was debated in some detail.

No official biography of Pater appeared during the decade, and the impulse towards a memoir was also vitiated. It has been suggested elsewhere that the Wilde trials may account for this.[16] Fears in Pater's sisters may also have been created by the religious controversies fanned by biographies. Moreover, Gosse, who had written a fairly full obituary for the *Contemporary Review* in 1894 and the *Dictionary of National Biography* life in 1895 was, by 1901, decidedly against the standard ritual of a two-volume tribute or "magnified epitaph" and may well have advised the sisters against such a project earlier. Similarly, it is unlikely from what A. C. Benson's diary and other sources reveal that Pater's Oxford colleagues, such as F. W. Bussell, Ingram Bywater, Lancelot Shadwell, and Benjamin Jowett, would welcome any scrutiny of their personal affairs. Why A. C. Benson who did not know Pater (although he probably had *seen* him) was asked by John Morley to write the English Men of Letters Pater is intriguing, and the answer may prove instructive. John Morley, it may be supposed, was favourably inclined toward Pater as he had published Pater's first signed article in the *Fortnightly* in 1869 and subsequent *Fortnightly Review* essays, and had written a tolerant review of *The Renaissance* in 1873.[17] Benson had been friends with Gosse from 1893, and Benson's biographer, David Newsome, suggests that it was as Gosse's protégé that Benson had been introduced into the London literary world.[18] Benson had his first English Men of Letters commission in 1903 for *Rossetti* (1904); a life of Edward Fitzgerald (1905) and the Pater volume (1906) followed.

In some respects Gosse seems a more suitable candidate for the biographer of Pater; he knew Pater well, and a respectable time had elapsed since the author's death. But perhaps in 1904 Gosse was unwilling to follow his own principle of indiscretion about a friend, and perhaps he recommended Benson to Morley. But it is also possible that Morley preferred Benson as a tried professional who had recently contributed two Lives of near contemporaries. Negative factors may have put him off Gosse, whose contributions to the second series of the English Men of Letters had been volumes on Jeremy Taylor (1903) and Sir Thomas Browne (1905), authors from an earlier period.[19] Moreover in 1886, Gosse's accuracy and degree of knowledge of literature had been scathingly attacked by J. C. Collins in a review of Gosse's *From Shakespeare to Pope* in the *Quarterly*,[20] in 1900 Charles Eliot Norton censured Gosse's *Life of Donne* for similar faults,[21] and a *TLS* reviewer reported that "the late Leonard Whibley used to say that the life of Gray [written for the *DNB* by Leslie Stephen who followed Gosse's biography of Gray so closely he felt like a thief] was not susceptible of correction; every sentence in it was incorrect, or inadequate, or misleading."[22] Either version of how Pater's biographer emerged is pertinent: if Gosse demurred because his first-hand knowledge of Pater, his "Widow" loyalty overcame his sense of professional responsibility, or if Morley chose Benson as the more professional of the two, in preference to Gosse's Widow posture. To what extent Benson is professional and to what extent protective remains to be seen.

That John Morley may have asked Benson rather than Gosse is possibly the cause of what is referred to by Benson in his diary as Gosse's self-confessed jealousy in November 1904:

> [G] Thought I was doing too much; ought to be silent for a bit. [He] Praised the Rossetti, + said it had made me a real position. I pointed out that I did my best, that my work was not hurried or particularly slipshod. That one must follow one's bent in the fruitful years; that he wrote much more than I did ... I don't think I converted him; but he said smiling 'Perhaps it is only jealousy, after all' – + we went in to lunch.[23]

This paragraph is then immediately followed by the second mention of Pater in the diary, which does not indicate in any more explicit way the date of Benson's arrangements with Macmillan for the Pater volume; but from this entry in November 1904 until 4 March, 1907, when Gosse shows Benson Thomas Wright's biography, Pater figures regularly in the diary. In January 1905 Benson talked with Oscar Browning about Pater; in May and in June he visits Oxford; on 30 May he visits Pater's sisters in London, plainly for the first time; he records that he began writing 31 May, and that he finished 25 August. He corrects proof in December, and the volume appears in May 1906. The diary shows the process by which Benson created the English Men of Letters life; it appears that he relied almost entirely on hearsay, on long discussions with those of Pater's intimates who would see him, and who were easily accessible in Oxford, Cambridge, or in London; for example, it appears from the diary that he never conferred with Ingram Bywater who retired from Oxford as Regius Professor of Greek in 1908. He appears to have seen only a few letters (Hester Pater writes in 1905 "Walter's letters are so rare – only a stray one here and there to be found"),[24] and to have confined his other research to a rapid survey of Pater's Oxford environment. His main sources were Gosse; Herbert Warren, President of Magdalen; Rev. F. W. Bussell, Vice-Principal and Tutor at BNC; Basil Champneys, architect and author; Douglas Ainslie, diplomat and writer; Clara and Hester Pater; Shadwell, Pater's friend and Literary Executor, and Oscar Browning. The Pater sisters and Shadwell were reticent and told him little of use, and

Oscar Browning, apart from leering "I was very intimate with him – he was very attached to me" could tell Benson nothing. After talking with two sources, Champneys and Bussell, Benson records that he immediately wrote up sections of the book. But Gosse, on the occasion of his jealousy in 1904, provides him with the basic information with which he can understand the reticence, the hints and innuendos, and the franker talk of his other sources. Gosse tells Benson "two things I didn't know":

> (1) that Pater's character was a good deal blown upon – that Jowett was said to have some mysterious letters, which he vowed he would produce if P. ever thought of standing for any University office. Probably some indiscreet devotion, Pateresquely expressed – for that Pater was ever anything but frigidly Platonic in his affections I decline to believe.[25]

and also that Pater was "the most secluded of men, the most *averse* to *action* – just desirous of garnering impressions, + filling the space of life, between the dark + the dark with colour + sweetness." Benson goes on to describe Pater, dejected, asking Gosse to write an article about him. After Oscar Browning and Gosse, Benson saw Dr Daniel, Provost of Worcester College, and Shadwell; the Daniels

> both talked of Pater, but saying much conveyed very little idea, except that he was humble, simple, easy to get on with. The Provost hinted at the dark chapter but I know all about that, + it will want great care.[26]

Herbert Warren of Magdalen College, Oxford talked of "the aesthetic movement, Symonds, Pater, Jowett, + others. Rather a dark place, I am afraid."[27] Benson makes explicit the connexion between aestheticism, Hellenism, and homosexuality, and between Pater and Symonds, but he also distinguishes between the two men:

> But if we give boys Greek books to read + hold up the Greek spirit + the Greek life as a marvel, it is very difficult to slice out one portion, which was a perfectly normal part of Greek life, and to say that it is abominable etc etc. A strongly sensuous nature – such as Pater or Symonds – with a strong instinct for beauty, + brought up at an English public school, will almost certainly go wrong, in thought if not in act. But Warren revealed to me a depth of corruption in Symonds of which I had not dreamed. When he was well + strong he remained free from the shadow.[28]

Also at Oxford, Shadwell "walked up + down discoursing of Pater for an hour, till I was giddy, + telling me nothing. But I got a faint impression."[29] From Pater's by then eccentric sisters Benson seems to have had little about Pater except their blessing on the project: "There is no one in whose hands we would rather see this. You will treat it justly + sympathetically."[30] But Benson notes: "I felt an even greater interest in my peep at this odd interior than even in Pater himself. ... the thought of the dim half-lit light, the faded + dreary atmosphere in which these two refined ladies sit, waiting for the end struck me as horribly pathetic + futile."[31] Likewise, when Benson visits Bussell in late June he echoes this greater interest in his source than in his object:

> I must say this Though I came in search of Pater, + though I found much that I wanted + desired, yet the discovery of Bussell has amused + interested me much more! Like a man who goes out to catch a rare + shy moth, + catches instead a rare + effusive butterfly.[32]

Benson's attitude to Pater might be described as mere mild interest. His searching is not very vigorous nor is his desire, and he is easily distracted. When the book appeared, Benson's response is repugnance:

> Gosse + Warren wrote in warm praise, of the book – which appeared yesterday [i.e. 11 May]. But the truth is that when a book comes out, so long has elapsed since one had anything to do with it, that it is like cold pie-crust. I open Pater, + the caked fat seems to stand on the gravy.[33]

This reveals something of Benson's depression and bouts of despair during the writing of the Pater life; he expresses it more explicitly in the entry for 24 June, 1905:

> I had mildly melancholy thoughts. Why do I achieve so little? Why do I give up practical life from a sincere diffidence + a sense of incompetence? and having done so why can I not write anything to my mind? I *can* write, but I have nothing to say, + when I say it sincerely, Cornish [Francis Warre, Vice-Provost of Eton] says it is rancid, + the Guardian that a character is revealed which one cannot sympathise with, or even respect! ... Some deep rooted weakness of will, no doubt – but I did not make my will! Who made it weak, + why?
>
> But I don't despair – I repent, I repent! I will try to do better, + I hope + believe I shall. It is useless to say 'Why are you so self-absorbed, with so narrow a view?' One may as well say to a lame man, 'Why is your leg crooked?' or to an ugly man 'Why is your face displeasing?'[34]

Benson's "sincere diffidence," his "weakness of will" is everywhere apparent in the diary, with respect to Pater. Benson seems to lack commitment to his task, and strong interest in his subject. Only once in the diary can he be said to enter imaginatively and feelingly into Pater's situation, in his last discussion with Gosse.

Bussell emerges as markedly less serious and austere, and more colourful than his memorial sermon on Pater suggests. He was, it seems, particularly good at imitating Pater, and this he did for Benson, who graphically describes his first sight of Bussell:

He looked like a man dressed for a garden party, as indeed he was. This was Bussell. Add to this an elaborately civil, slightly simpering, slightly giggling, infectious, humorous, ironical, *petting*, caressing kind of manner – (like Gosse in the mood I do not think his best) – as a smooth + engaging – but not wholly trustworthy – cat might play + bound about you, + you have this singular man. He is very able, very accomplished.[35]

The rest of the long diary entry on Bussell reveals nothing about Pater directly – only implicitly through its portraits of Bussell and Shadwell. After Benson's visits with Bussell and the sisters, Benson indicates that he made notes. On 10 June he talked with Basil Champneys who was "highly illuminating" about Pater because he didn't "shirk the unpleasant side."[36] Champneys pleased Benson "by saying that he was deeply thankful that the truth was in discreet hands."

In July Benson visited Douglas Ainslie for an hour. Curiously, this entry shows Benson's limitations as well as Ainslie's: a kind of aesthetic snobbery; a taste for "good + wholesome work" and a tendency to indulge in self-contradiction, without examining what lies behind the paradoxes:

Sunday 11 July   The heat was awful. Arrived in town I went straight to Mount Street + had an hour's interview with Douglas Ainslie, aged about 35, dramatic critic, poet, + ex diplomatist, about Pater. How I hate the sort of room he lived in – many books + evidently well-read; but semi-artistic things about – the whole thing dusty + a little pretentious – no *grace* – + then the noise + stench of London pouring in at the window. How can good + wholesome work be done under these conditions. He told me some interesting things about P. But seemed to me too anxious to get himself mentioned. I thought him a clever man, of much aesthetic perception; but all in the outer rooms + corridors of art. I should not trust his judgment for an instant. He would easily mistake secondrate for firstrate. .. I thought him *very* kind, rather clever, rather graceful, not impressive.[37]

The first mention of Pater in the diary shows Benson, in 1902, to be offended by Pater's taste for ritual in *Marius*:

Today I actually had but 3 letters; so I read Marius the Epicurean + tasted its luscious sentences deliberately – but Pater's taste for *ritual* offends me – there is something radically silly I think in the assembling dressed up for solemn ceremonial. It is rather impressive when you drop in upon it, + don't know the people; but to do it with people one knows, over + over again seems to me truly absurd.[38]

It reveals a temperamental intolerance of a persistent element of Pater's prose and life. Elsewhere in the diary Benson contrasts Pater (among others) with a precious visitor who was translating Baudelaire:

> The strange squire of John's to lunch – in pumps! – the day being wet; hair in curled masses, + with a gold chain round his waist. He is a confirmed *poseur*, I fear. He said he had been applying for a tutorship to prepare a little boy for school, his real object being to get leisure to finish a translation of *Baudelaire*! How good for the little boy to be under this influence.

> I am very sorry for him – I think he has many pretty thoughts – but he is morbid; corrupt, hysterical. We talked of Pater; + I read S a concealed lecture on the absurdity of *personal* eccentricity, + how the masters, like Pater, Pusey, Ruskin abhorred all formal preciousness in life etc.[39]

Such a wrenched reading of Pater who wore an apple green tie and whose eccentricity, if quiet, appears highly personal, indicates the lacunae in Benson's concept of Pater; they are reflected at one point in the biography where Benson characterises Pater's ideal of life as "sober + strenuous."[40] On 28 August, three days after he finished writing, Benson rejects H. E. Luxmoore's "ugly Puritanism" about Pater; to his friend's contention "that Pater was a dangerous man, corrupt + vile when he was at Oxford," Benson "interposed, + said that he was reckless at first but became different, very different in later life":[41] this is one expression of Benson's personal beliefs about Pater at the point of his finishing the biography – that Pater *had* been "reckless" early on but that he changed.

Finally, on 1 September, having "FINISHED PATER" on 25 August, Benson records that Gosse revealed that "it was *Mallock* who took the terrible letters to Jowett, which gave Jowett such power." Benson here affords us more of his final estimate of Pater; and a rare sign of empathy with his subject.

> What a donkey P. must have been to *write* them – it is a mistake one makes to feel that writing is somehow more impersonal than speech – It is: but it is also imperishable!

> Pater's whole nature changed under the strain, after the dreadful interview with Jowett. He became old, crushed, despairing – + this dreadful weight lasted for years; it was years before he realised that J. would not use them. And then came the time when Jowett, finding P. famous, called, when Pater was ill to enquire. J. was a little hypocrite, I fear; or at all events a vile little opportunist.[42]

It seems clear that, even after Benson had done his research and written the book, he had not known that Mallock was Jowett's supplier until Gosse told him in September. His research seems precariously thin, and when he was accused of inaccuracy by Thomas Wright, he blames his informants:

> There is a very severe + nasty attack on my book. This only moved me with a faint discomfort. All my facts were got from the nearest friends + relations, + *I am not responsible for my errors*. But I expect I shall have to answer him.[43]

In the light of what Benson knew about Pater, his 'speculations' about Pater and Jowett in the English Men of Letters volume appear positively disingenuous:

> Although Pater had been a pupil of Jowett's and although there was a *rapprochement* in later life, when Jowett took occasion warmly to congratulate Pater on his *Plato and Platonism*, there was a misunderstanding of some kind which resulted in a dissidence between them in the middle years. It has even been said that Jowett took up a line of definite opposition to Pater, and used his influence to prevent his obtaining University work and appointments. It is not impossible that this was the case. Jowett, in spite of his genius, in spite of his liberality of view and his deliberate tolerance, was undoubtedly an opportunist. He was not exactly guided by the trend of public opinion, but he took care not to back men or measures unless he would be likely to have the support of a strong section of the community, or at least conceived it probable that his line would eventually be endorsed by public opinion ...
>
> Probably Jowett either identified Pater with the advanced aesthetic school, or supposed that at all events his teaching was adapted to strengthen a species of Hedonism, or modern Paganism, which was alien to the spirit of the age. Or possibly he was alarmed at the mental and moral attitude with which Pater was publicly credited, owing in considerable measure to the appearance of the *New Republic* – in which he himself was pilloried as the representative of advanced religious liberalism – and thought that on public grounds he must combat the accredited leaders of a movement which was certainly unfashionable, and which was regarded with suspicion by men of practical minds. Whatever his motives were, he certainly meant to make it plain that he did not desire to see the supposed exponents of the aesthetic philosophy holding office in the University.
>
> One feels that Jowett, with his talent for frank remonstrance, had better have employed direct rather than indirect methods; but the fact remains that he not only disliked the tendency of Pater's thought, but endeavoured, by means that are invariably ineffectual, to subvert his influence.[44]

Benson misleads his readers in that he implies the principal responsibility for the rift lay with Jowett; he implies the direct involvement of Mallock but displaces it. His tentativeness and multiple speculations are careful structures of deceit. And yet it must be acknowledged that Benson says more here than anyone else before him. In November 1906 Benson notes G.T. Lapsley's account of Basil Champneys' praise:

> 'I took my courage in my hands, thinking it the only thing to do, + told Benson a mass of impossible things about Pater, hoping he wd be discreet. But he was more discreet than I cd have hoped – he

discovered the man behind it all, he committed no indiscretions, +
yet one who knows the whole story can see that B[enson] knows it
too.' This was high praise + pleased me very much.[45]

Champneys' view no doubt reflects relief from guilt, but it also indicates
the full *extent* of Benson's discretion. Benson's satisfaction with the
notion of two audiences is notable: one élite in the know, and the other
vulgarly public, forever excluded from the fuller private life. But does the
EML Life merit such praise? In 1906 Robert Ross published a review of
Benson's volume in the *Academy*. [46] Ross had been a close friend of Oscar
Wilde, and had remained openly loyal to him during the trials and his
imprisonment; Ross published *De Profundis*. He was also a close friend of
Gosse, and clearly knew the details of Pater's life to which Gosse and
Benson were privy.[47] At the beginning of the review Ross pays tribute to
the author's "sympathy and critical acumen," but towards the end he
considers critically Benson's method of deriving the life from the self-
revelatory works – which he prefers to Benson's use of empty personal
anecdotes. But in both of these, Ross detects concealment, and he indicates Mallock ("the horrid undergraduate") as analogous to Henley on
Stevenson and Burns, and Purcell on Manning, ready to ink the statue.
Ross also suggests Benson is guilty of deliberate misleading:

> Anticipating something of the kind, Mr. Benson is careful to insist
> on the divergence between Rossetti and Pater, and on page 86 says
> something which is ludicrously untrue.

What Benson writes there is "the innermost world of mystical passion in
which Rossetti lived was as a locked and darkened chamber to Pater."
Ross defends what Purcell had called "the publication of historical facts."
Gosse writes somewhat ambiguously and pompously to Ross about the
review on 8 November, 1906:

> My dear Robbie ...
>   What is peculiar to your own mind and nature comes out most
> agreeably here and there, and I hope you will cultivate it. The article
> on Pater is excellently written, and with the greater part of it I agree.
> I do not know that I mind the end. That is a sound expression of
> opinion, and I do not feel that it goes too far.[48]

Gosse, the vociferous defender of indiscreet biography, supplies Benson
with the material for such a biography, but ambivalently – in stages, and
late; he then patronises its reviewer and only reluctantly tolerates his
detection of Benson's discretion.[49] Benson's life of Pater fails even to
mention Pater's friendships with Simeon Solomon, Oscar Browning,
Wilde, and Jackson. Edward Lyttleton, Benson's friend from 1884, when
Benson went to teach at Eton notes Benson's

> want of interest in questions of principle; the effect of which is to
> enfeeble the grip on fact, or at least – if the memory is strong – to
> prevent the mind from seeing facts in their true proportion. Arthur's

memory was good enough; but the deep motives of human action, the interplay of the forces which stir the mass-movements of man-kind, no less than the mighty drama of human souls in their period of probation, remained outside his horizon. So the facts which, to some minds, speak of these and great kindred matters presented themselves to him without colour or any rich significance.[50]

This is a view put by the *Athenaeum* reviewer of Benson's *Rossetti* who noted that work's superficiality; and it seems a good description of what Benson's diffidence, and his fear of depths, of darkness, engendered. It is interesting that in 1910 in the only known letter between Benson and Ross, Benson did not seem to begrudge Ross the review. The author thanks the critic for a favourable review of his latest book, noting the "finely discriminating hand," "sympathetic praise," and the "urbanity" in the review; he also acknowledges that though they have never met, they have "many common friends."[51]

Benson, Gosse, and Ross then all had access to information in 1906 which could have obviated the considerable efforts in twentieth-century criticism of Pater to determine the reasons behind both critical and biographical problems: the withdrawal of the Conclusion from the 1877 edition of *The Renaissance*; the necessity for the apparent disjunction between the life and the work; the apparently repressed character and life; the outbreaks of vivid and vehement expression in the work; and the paucity of letters and other biographical material. These three critics all sympathised with Pater's predicament, but they had differing notions of responsible biography: Gosse preached indiscretion but remained silent himself; Ross was less mealy-mouthed; he exposed Benson's evasive methods, but only indicated where the full truth lay. But Benson, the professional biographer, seems torn; his tendency to research super-ficially, and his failure to value sufficiently "the deep motives of human action" combine to produce a misleading, widow biography, but at the same time Benson's personal pre-occupation with a succession of roman-tic friendships does enable him at times to indicate in the Life his apprecia-tion of Pater's situation with Jowett. Benson, in his combination of widow and professional, conflates the terms which Gosse opposed.

Henry James, in an article on George Sand in 1897,[52] foresees a future in which "the pale forewarned victim" of biography will be a match for "the cunning of the inquirer" "with every track covered, every paper burnt and every letter unanswered." To Benson, James wrote, in June 1906 on the occasion of the book, of Pater as a "figure";

You have done in especial *this* delightful + interesting thing – that you have ministered to that strange touching edifying (to me quite thrilling) operation of the whispering of time, through which Pater has already in these few years, little as he seemed marked out for it – become in our literature that very rare + sovereign thing, a *figure* : a figure in the sense in which there are to[o] few! It is a matter altogether independent of the mere possession of genius or achievement, even of 'success', I think. It's a matter almost of tragic or ironic (or even comic) felicity – but it comes here and there to the individual – unaware; it leaves hundreds of the eminent alone. Well I feel that it has come to dear, queer, deeply individual and homogeneous W. H. P. crowning his strong and painful identity.[53]

In the difference between James' brief and suggestive evocation and Benson's ultimately reticent narrative, we can see something of what Benson has denied us. In 1926 Benson published a piece on "The Art of the Biographer" in which he described his notion of the biographer's "business." It articulates aspects of the method implicit in the Pater biography, and also points to its dearth of "patience, energy and research." He provides his own best 'apologia' with all its tensions and value-judgments:

> He must have a relentless and microscopic faculty of observation; he must have patience, energy and research; he must have a power of omission and selection; and lastly he must have an extreme veraciousness, which does not pay any particular heed to decorum or sentiment or romance. He need not violate privacy or sacredness, anymore than a portrait painter need insist on always painting from the nude; but he must have no deference for the kind of hero-worship which requires that a man should be exhibited in flawless, stainless and radiant perfection, while his sympathy and reverence will save him from mere caricature and from undue emphasis on what was merely occasional, exaggerated or sensational. Proportion is the true difficulty; how to balance what is lofty, noble and awe-inspiring with what is minute, whimsical, humorous. Even what, as Rossetti beautifully said 'is secret and unknown below the earth, above the skies,' must, if not told, at least be able to be inferred ... the best biographer must know by a kind of inspired tact what is essential.[54]

Benson knew that books "always make me put on my company manners,"[55] and beyond them he could not, and did not go. He reveals his overwhelming consciousness of the necessity of discretion and of pleasing Pater's circle in the throes of his satisfaction with the quality of his writing: "Was in by five + wrote a chapter of Pater on Champneys notes. It is good work, I think; but will Shadwell approve."[56] Thomas Wright cannot be said to have suffered from *that* limitation, and in certain respects – the vigour of his information gathering, for example, and his use of letters – he could be regarded as the more professional of the two biographers, and if not a widow, not Judas either.

LAUREL BRAKE
University College of Wales, Aberystwyth

NOTES

1. Edmund Gosse, "The Ethics of Biography," *Cosmopolitan*, 35 (1903), 322. Hereafter "Ethics."
2. Edmund Gosse, "The Custom of Biography," *Anglo-Saxon Review* 8 (1901), 205-6. Hereafter "Custom."
3. The relation between these biographies is discussed by Thomas Wright in Vol. I of *The Life of Walter Pater* as one of rivalry, and this is echoed by the press. In Brasenose Library is a frigid letter from Lancelot Shadwell, Provost of Oriel, denying Wright information from himself and Pater's sisters. As the letter is dated 26 July, 1903, and as A.C. Benson's diary implies a later commencement of his professional interest in Pater (12 November, 1904), it is possible that the threat of a Judas biography resulted in efforts by Pater's family, friends, and publishers to organise a safe, 'widow' Life. See also Wright's explanation in his *Autobiography* of his experiences with Pater's friends and relations, and also with Benson, who in May 1905 is alleged by Wright to have offered payment to see Wright's Pater material and the manuscript of his biography.
4. Oscar Wilde, "The Butterfly's Boswell," *Court and Society Review* 4 (1887), 378.
5. Edmund Purcell, "On the Ethics of Suppression in Biography," *Nineteenth Century*, 40 (1896), 534-5.
6. "Concerning Biography," *Academy*, 60 (1901), 168.
7. "Custom," 195.
8. "Concerning Biography," 167.
9. "Ethics," 323.
10. "Ethics," 322.
11. "Ethics," 322.
12. *Spectator* 93 (13 August, 1904), 225.
13. *Athenaeum* (13 August, 1904), 197.
14. Leslie Stephen, "Biography," *National Review*, 22 (1893), 178-9.
15. "Biography," 175.
16. Michael Levey, *The Case of Walter Pater* (London: Thames and Hudson, 1978), pp. 20-1.
17. I say "tolerant" because in 1866 Morley published anonymously in the *Saturday Review* (4 August, 1866, 145-7) such a vituperative review of Swinburne's poems that the publishers withdrew the book from circulation. Morley's review of Pater in 1873, by which time he had clearly changed his mind about aestheticism, appeared in the *Fortnightly Review*, 13 (April 1873), 469-77. However, F.W. Hirst, in *Early Life and Letters of John Morley* (London: Macmillan, 1927), quotes a portion of a letter from Morley to Frederick Harrison which shows Morley to be tolerant of Pater's "transgressions":
    > I think it very desirable to call attention to any book like Pater's, which is likely to quicken public interest in the higher sorts of literature. And, moreover, a young and unknown writer like him ought to be formally introduced to the company by the hired master of the ceremonies, myself, or another to wit. So pray pardon my light dealing with his transgressions. (Vol. I, p. 240)
18. David Newsome, *On the Edge of Paradise. A.C. Benson: The Diarist* (London: John Murray, 1980), p. 88. Hereafter, Newsome.
19. Gosse *had* already written one EML volume for Morley on Gray in 1882 in the first series, but only one, and was to do the DNB and EML Swinburnes in 1912 and 1917.
20. [J.C. Collins] "From Shakespeare to Pope," *Quarterly Review*, 163 (1886), 289-329.
21. C.E. Norton, "Gosse's Life of Donne," *Nation*, 70 (8 and 15 February, 1900), 111-13, 133-5.
22. *TLS* (16 December, 1949), 819.
23. A.C. Benson, MS Diary, Vol. 62 (12 November, 1904), p. 4. Hereafter, all references to Benson's Diary will be cited as *Diary*. I wish to thank the Master and fellows of

Magdalene College, Cambridge for permission to quote from this diary.

24. *Letters of Walter Pater*, ed. L. Evans (London: OUP, 1970), p. 157.
25. *Diary*, 62 (12 November, 1904), 5r-5v.
26. *Diary*, 69 (18 May, 1905), 47v.
27. *Diary*, 69 (18 May, 1905), 48v-49r.
28. *Diary*, 69 (18 May, 1905), 49r.
29. *Diary*, 69 (19 May, 1905), 52r.
30. *Diary*, 70 (30 May, 1905), 7v.
31. *Diary*, 70 (30 May, 1905), 8r-8v.
32. *Diary*, 71 (24 June, 1905), 27v.
33. *Diary*, 81 (12 May, 1906), 69r.
34. *Diary*, 71 (2[5] June, 1905), 30r. Although dated 24 June in the *Diary*, the entry appears, from the designation "Sunday," to have been written on the 25th.
35. *Diary*, 71 (24 June, 1905), 19v-20r.
36. *Diary*, 70 (10 June, 1905), 33r.
37. *Diary*, 71 (11 July, 1905), 77v-78r.
38. *Diary*, 17 (26 August, 1902), 42r.
39. *Diary*, 82 (26 May, 1906), 24r-24v.
40. A. C. Benson, *Walter Pater* (London: Macmillan, 1906), p. 54.
41. *Diary*, 73 (28 August, 1905), 57r.
42. *Diary*, 73 (1 September, 1905), 66r.
43. *Diary*, 90 (4 March, 1907), 44r. my italics.
44. A. C. Benson, *Walter Pater* (London: Macmillan, 1906), pp. 54-5.
45. *Diary*, 87 (2 November, 1906), 1.
46. *Academy*, 71 (1906), 61-2.
47. Cf. Letter from Edmund Gosse to Robert Ross in *Robert Ross, Friend of Friends*, ed. Margery Ross (London: Cape, 1952), pp. 132-3.
48. *Robert Ross, Friend of Friends*, p. 132. Gosse's pomposity regarding Ross and homosexuality is nowhere more apparent than in his letter to Ross during the Wilde trials; cf. *Friend of Friends*, pp. 36-7.
49. In this connexion Harold Nicolson's judgment of the nature of Gosse's biographies, other than *Father and Son*, is pertinent; see *The Development of English Biography*, 1928 (1968 impression), p. 144 where he writes:
    Sir Edmund Gosse has relieved the pressure of facts, the explosive force of the scientific elements, by the safety valve of innuendo. . . . while not defying truth, he allows the external pressure of truth to evaporate and to escape. These works will for long remain as models of grace and dexterity, but they will not live as models of biography.
50. E. Lyttelton, "Training and Temperament," in *Arthur Christopher Benson. As Seen by Some Friends* (London: G. Bell & Sons, 1925), p. 154.
51. Letter (20 September, 1910) from A. C. Benson to Robert Ross in *Robert Ross, Friend of Friends*, p. 187.
52. Henry James, "George Sand," *The Yellow Book*, 12 (1897), 23.
53. *Diary*, 82 (1 June, 1906), 40r.
54. A. C. Benson, "The Art of the Biographer" in *Essays by Divers Hands* (London: OUP., 1926) 163-4.
55. Newsome, p. 10.
56. *Diary*, 70 (10 June, 1905), 34r.

Pater and Ruskin on Michelangelo: Two Contrasting Views

In 1871 Ruskin delivered one of the most notorious lectures of his career. It was entitled "The Relation Between Michael Angelo and Tintoret" and in it Ruskin described Michelangelo as "the chief captain in evil" of the Italian Renaissance.[1] He was, said Ruskin, "proud, yet not proud enough to be at peace; melancholy, yet not deeply enough to be raised above petty pain."[2] Ruskin gave this lecture in the University Museum Galleries, Oxford, on 13 June, 1871, and only five months later another account of the artist appeared from the pen of an Oxford critic. In November 1871 Pater published "The Poetry of Michelangelo" in the *Fortnightly Review*[3] but it was quite unlike Ruskin's denunciation of the evil genius of the Renaissance. Pater's stress on Michelangelo's sensitivity and inner psychological struggle elicited the comment from John Addington Symonds that Pater had a "delicate sympathy" with Michelangelo's mind.[4] Inevitably, one wonders whether Pater who was in Oxford in June 1871[5] heard Ruskin's lecture at a time when he was certainly composing his own ideas on the subject. We know that Ruskin's views created a disturbance. Edward Poynter, the Slade Professor at London University said that he burned "with indignation" when he heard about them;[6] Sir William Richmond, Ruskin's successor in the Oxford chair, tried to undo the harm he felt that Ruskin had done by delivering a eulogy on Michelangelo's work in the Sistine Chapel,[7] and rather more impulsively Edward Burne Jones, when he was told how Ruskin had treated one of his artistic heroes, said that he thought of taking to drink or drowning himself in the Surrey Canal.[8] There is, however, no direct evidence that Pater was aware of Ruskin's performance. He makes no mention of Ruskin's name in his essay and there is no quotation from Ruskin's lecture. Yet when one looks more closely at the two pieces there are a number of thematic similarities between them, and there is something in Pater's rather oblique approach to Michelangelo which suggests that he might have had Ruskin in mind. For example, both critics make substantial use of the collection of Michelangelo drawings in the possession of the University. Ruskin claimed that it was his duty to warn students that "these designs have nothing whatever to do with present life, with its passions, or with its religion."[9] On the contrary, says Pater, one of the reasons for studying Michelangelo is that he helps us to unravel "the mixed, confused productions of the modern mind."[10] It is through the clearer outlines of Michelangelo, says Pater, that we can understand the more complex work of William Blake or Victor Hugo. Again Ruskin makes a great deal of what he calls Michelangelo's "bad workmanship"[11] – the lack of finish and the incompleteness of some of the sculpture. Pater, however, draws attention to this incompleteness as one of Michelangelo's most beguiling characteristics. On one occasion he says that the lack of finish is Michelangelo's equivalent for colour; on another he says that it is Michelangelo's way of identifying the sculptured figure with the living rock from which it is hewn. In these studies of Michelangelo there are four important questions raised by both Ruskin and Pater on which they differ significantly. They both discuss the status of the show of strength and power in Michelangelo's art; they both speak of the part Michelangelo was supposed to have played first in the Renaissance then in the Counter Reformation; both of them test his treatment of the nude against the standards of classical Greece; and both of them invoke the temperament of Michelangelo to support their critical theories. On these issues Pater makes no attempt to refute Ruskin directly. He treads warily around the questions of morality for example. Instead, Pater presents his readers with a different view of Michelangelo. Where Ruskin describes him as bombastic, mannered and overblown, Pater depicts him as a character of gentle melancholy disposition and above all "sweet." It may seem curious that two such different portraits of Michelangelo could be drawn within six months of each other, yet the whole history of Michelangelo criticism is one of disagreement. Though both these portraits now seem to us slightly eccentric neither of them is entirely fictional. They both have their basis in fact; both of them rely upon a number of received ideas and both of them represent the extension of a long standing debate about the nature of Michelangelo and his work.

Michelangelo had never been the subject of neglect. Unlike the work of Botticelli or that of Piero della Francesca no one could overlook the *Last Judgement* in the Sistine Chapel or ignore the sculpture in the Medici Chapel in Florence. All visitors to Rome were forced to pass some judgement on St Peter's. Familiarity with Michelangelo's work, however, did not promote agreement, and from the time that Vasari published his eloquent praise of Michelangelo in *The Lives of ... the Painters* in 1568 voices of dissent had been raised. According to Vasari the history of art before Michelangelo was a prelude to his magnificence; Michelangelo, he said, was a divine gift to the aesthetically benighted human race; he was the saviour of the arts and the prince of artists. Understandably there was a reaction to this extreme point of view, and it was one which grew strongly in the seventeenth century. Malvasia and Bellori both wrote histories of painting which contained the sharp reminder that both Bologna and Rome had produced artists of outstanding merit;[12] the Venetian writers Scanelli and Lomazzo pointed out that Titian far excelled Michelangelo in the art of oil painting,[13] and the artist Salvator Rosa wrote a rhyming essay which satirised Michelangelo in favour of Neapolitan painting.[14] The seventeenth-century writers Roland Fréart and John Evelyn attacked Michelangelo in two ways. They objected to his scriptural heterodoxy (Christ and Charon in the same picture) and to what they felt to be his licentiousness.[15] Strange though it now seems, there was a period in the early eighteenth century when the moral condemnation of Michelangelo was very strong. In 1722, for example, Jonathan Richardson retrospectively congratulated the "breeches-maker" Daniele da Volterra, on covering up what Richardson called the "choquing Improprieties" of the Sistine Chapel.[16]

The later eighteenth century saw what might be called a conflict over the beautiful and the sublime in Michelangelo's art. Led by Winckelmann, a group of writers decided that when measured against the standards of human beauty established in ancient Greece, Michelangelo's work was turbulent and mannered. Michelangelo lacked "decorum" and "grace," and his love of theatrical gesture anticipated the wild, violent postures of Baroque art which Winckelmann so hated. "The very course which led Michelangelo to impassible places and steep cliffs," wrote Winckelmann, "plunged Bernini ... into bogs and pools; for he sought to dignify as it were by exaggeration."[17] In England, however, Edmund Burke's theory of the sublime came to Michelangelo's aid. Burke does not actually mention Michelangelo, but even before Joshua Reynolds' eloquent defence of his hero in the famous *Discourses* the appreciation of Michelangelo's art had become closely connected with feelings of magnificence and of terror.[18] Reynolds himself had little use for continental theories like those of Winkelmann and was happy to breathe Michelangelo's name as the last word in his last lecture as President of the Royal Academy.[19] With various reservations and modifications, the tradition that Michelangelo's work represented a sublime moment in the history of art was perpetuated in this country by the lectures of the academicians John Opie and Henry Fuseli. In his fifth lecture at the Royal Academy, Fuseli, subtly changing a metaphor from Winkelmann, said, "The breadth of Michelangelo resembles the tide and ebb of a mighty sea: waves approach, arrive, retreat, but in their rise and fall ... impress us only with the image of the power that raises, that directs them."[20] In a lecture of 1784 James Barry introduced the adjective "Michelangelesque,"[21] meaning "sublime," into the language, and ten years later the same tradition was set to not very accomplished verse by John Courtney who asked: "But who with Angelo can vie?"

> He rears his wondrous dome on high
>   Pois'd in the ethereal clime
> His daring pencil boasts the art
>   To awe the eye, to rule the heart
> And paint the true sublime.[22]

In the nineteenth century a new challenge to the supremacy of Michelangelo in England came from the devotees of early Italian art. The primitives were valued for their simplicity, their restraint and their understatement. What then of Michelangelo? What place could be found for him in the new interpretation of the history of art which put so much emphasis on the sentiment, piety and morality of medievalism? Ruskin and Pater gave different answers to this problem. For Ruskin, Michelangelo was wholly unworthy because he provided aesthetic expression for a decadent culture – in his words for the "partly scientific and completely lascivious enthusiasms of literature and painting, renewed under classical influence."[23] Pater, however, stressed Michelangelo's links with the earlier phases of art which had become so popular in the early nineteenth century; Michelangelo, he said, was the final flowering of the medieval spirit. "He sums up," said Pater, "the whole character of medieval art ... in that which distinguishes it most clearly from classical work."[24]

So each century after Michelangelo's death had contributed some new element to the debate about the value of his work. One question, however, dominated all others – what do we make of the extravagant show of power and strength in the work? Pater was aware of this difficulty and confronted it in the first sentence of his essay. "Critics of Michelangelo," he said, "have sometimes spoken as if the only characteristic of his genius were a wonderful strength, verging ... on what is singular or strange."[25] This was quite true. Writers from Richardson at the beginning of the eighteenth century to Fuseli at the end were obsessed by the magnificence and power of Michelangelo to the exclusion of other subtler qualities. "There is not a more remarkable example of ... the force of the sublime than that of Michelangelo"[26] said Richardson, and according to Fuseli, Michelangelo made "beauty of form" subservient to "grandeur."[27] Comparing Michelangelo with Raphael, Reynolds said that Michelangelo "has more of the Poetical Inspiration; his ideas are vast and sublime,"[28] and in William Brown's 1770 translation of Lodovico Dolce's *Dialogue on Painting* the strength of Michelangelo is compared to that of the sun which "not only surpasses, but extinguishes every other light."[29] William Wordsworth combined the well-established idea of Michelangelo as the Homer of the Renaissance[30] with Dolce's view of him as the great light of the sixteenth century when he confessed to Thomas Landseer in 1824 that Michelangelo

> is the great epic painter, the poet executing his high imaginings with the pencil; no one touches the hem of his garment in that lofty comprehensiveness that soars beyond the regions of commonplace, adding ideality and greatness to ordinary forms, giving sublimity and distinctive character to what in other hands might only be dramatic. ... we must brace the sinews, so to speak of our comprehension to grapple with the grandeur and sublimity of thought and imagination, the epic greatness, of Michael Angelo, who has the merit of eclipsing ... every other artist that had preceded him; – I mean of that epoch. And we must not forget that it was the splendour, the brilliance, the superlative lustre of this sun of Art, that shone, and enlightened with new and ennobling impressions and enlarged conceptions the refined, pure intelligence and the beautiful soul – if I am permitted to say so, – of Raphael. The brighter luminary glanced, as it were, a ray of its peculiar force to the already divinely endowed genius, and added a new lustre to that already there.[31]

With hints of Shakespeare's *Henry V* ("We must brace the sinews") Wordsworth's view of Michelangelo sums up a number of late-eighteenth century attitudes to the artist. For Wordsworth, as for so many of his contemporaries, Michelangelo's power set him apart from his fellows. Nurtured on Vasari's insistence on the uniqueness of Michelangelo, Wordsworth sees Raphael as the prism whose existence is dependent upon the sun of the Renaissance. For Wordsworth, Michelangelo is an isolated genius whose achievement he describes in a number of imprecise terms, and he makes no attempt to place Michelangelo in the history of art. During the early years of the nineteenth century this was to change. A number of important studies of Michelangelo were written in which there was a real attempt to locate the massive grandeur of his art in the social and political conditions of the Renaissance. One of the first writers to explain Michelangelo like this was Michael Scott, the painter and brother of William Bell Scott. In a long account of Michelangelo's *Last Judgement* written for *Blackwood's Magazine* in 1839, Scott placed what he called "the great epic of expectation and dread" firmly in the context of the art and life of its day.[32] "The great fresco," he said, "is eminently a portion of the time in which it was produced,"[33] and he shows how the picture is related to Renaissance violence on one hand and theological controversy on the other. The theological aspects of the *Last Judgement* presented peculiar problems for the nineteenth-century critic. Scott explains the power of the picture in terms of a particularly violent phase of Catholicism, whereas Lord Lindsay, the author of *Sketches of the History of Christian Art* (1847), turns it into a great Protestant epic. In his view Michelangelo's "terror" was didactic; he was, in Lindsay's words, the "representative of the Protestant spirit within the bosom of Catholicism."[34] It was the French, however, who did most to promote Michelangelo as a superman. Stendhal, Delacroix, Baudelaire, Quinet, Michelet and Taine all contributed to the idea that Michelangelo was a wild and eccentric Renaissance giant whose works embodied the relentless struggle of historical forces.[35] "It is not grace that one admires," wrote Delacroix in 1830, "it seems [Michelangelo] never thought of pleasing ... he invents ... to dominate the imagination ... to present the mind with menacing and frightening images."[36] In Michelet and Taine this romantic view of Michelangelo reached an absurd pitch of intensity. So great was Michelangelo's power that as Michelet entered the Vatican he felt "the walls and the vaults of the Sistine Chapel trembling with terror," while Hippolyte Taine, also in the Sistine Chapel, was overwhelmed by the "thundering voice" which reverberated about him.[37] Ruskin inherited the Romantic view of Michelangelo's strength, but inverted the values that had become attached to it. Where French writers saw his power as the clearest evidence of his genius, Ruskin identified it with his decadence. Michelangelo, says Ruskin, "is strong beyond all his companion workmen, yet never strong enough to command his temper or limit his aims."[38] He describes him as an athlete in a High Renaissance circus, then, perhaps most cutting of all, attacks his devotees. "His ostentatious display of

strength and science," says Ruskin, "has a natural attraction for comparatively weak and pedantic persons."[39] It is small wonder that Pater directs
his reader's attention away from the violence and strength of Michelangelo to what he calls his "sweetness." While Ruskin describes Michelangelo as a powerful champion of the Counter-Reformation, Pater
refuses to see him as the strong man of the sixteenth century. Speaking of
this period in his life, Pater says that "he lingers on; a *revenant*, as the
French say, a ghost out of another age."[40] The important phrase here is
"out of another age," for it is in tracing the roots of Michelangelo's art that
Pater creates the most convincing alternative to Ruskin's empty strong-
man. "He must be approached," says Pater, "not through his followers,
but through his predecessors; not through the marbles of St Peter's, but
through the work of the sculptors of the fifteenth century over the tombs
and altars of Tuscany."[41] Again and again Pater emphasises Michelangelo's debt to the Middle Ages. "He comes," says Pater, "with a genius
spiritualised by the reveries of the middle age, penetrated by its spirit of
inwardness and introspection."[42] The true Michelangelo says Pater is to
be found not in sixteenth-century demonstrativeness but in the quieter,
subtler inheritance of fifteenth-century expressiveness. Pater's idea is a
highly original one. Until the mid-nineteenth century critics had said little
or nothing about Michelangelo's debt to the past. The standard view was
still that of Vasari who claimed that Michelangelo had no equals and no
predecessors. According to Vasari, Signorelli had played John the Baptist
to Michelangelo's Christ, yet Signorelli was a pale anticipation of what
was to come.[43] This idea persisted well into the nineteenth century mainly
because there was very little systematic knowledge about Italian sculpture
of the fifteenth century. The work of the sculptors who so intrigued Pater
– Mino da Fiesole, Jacopo della Quercia, Giovanni da Pisa and Lucca
della Robbia – had been almost totally overlooked. For example, as late as
1826, in his outline of the development of western sculpture, John Flaxman could say that "we may ... pass over the intermediate names between
Donatello and Michelangelo as having added little to the value of modern
sculpture."[44] This view, popularised by Michelangelo's early nineteenth-
century biographer Quatremère de Quincy,[45] was not without its oppo-
nents on the continent. The Italian historian of sculpture Leopold Cicognara and the French writer Gustave Garrison both felt its inadequacy,[46]
but the historical ground-work was lacking and it was not until the work of
J.C. Robinson and Charles C. Perkins in this country that informed
connections between Michelangelo and his predecessors were at all possible.

The serious study of fifteenth-century sculpture was initiated by the
purchase of the Gherardini Collection in 1854, by the South Kensington
Museum. In 1862 the museum put on a special exhibition where the
works of Jacopo della Quercia, Mino da Fiesole, Donatello and Lucca
della Robbia could, for the first time, be compared with a cupid that in
Pater's day was thought to be by Michelangelo. As the curator, J.C.
Robinson, wrote in his catalogue, Michelangelo's "nervous chisel was

inspired by the accumulated power, the distinctive originality, and, in a word, by all the achievement of quattro-cento art."[47] It was, however, Charles Perkins' internationally famous book, *Tuscan Sculptors* of 1864 that put these artists for the first time in their historical perspective. For Pater this was the only reliable authority on fifteenth-century sculpture, and he undoubtedly used it in describing Michelangelo's debt to the work of Jacopo della Quercia in Bologna. Perkins says:

> Those reliefs representing the creation of Eve and the expulsion from Paradise, are almost identical in treatment with the frescoes of the same subject painted by Raphael in the Vatican Loggia, and by Michael Angelo in the ceiling of the Sistine Chapel. As we know that Michael Angelo twice visited Bologna, and that his second visit took place only one year before he commenced the frescoes of the Sistine Chapel, we may fairly suppose that Quercia's works had made a strong impression upon him; nor can we wonder at this, since there is so evident an affinity between the two artists.[48]

And Pater, using the same facts, recreates Michelangelo's experience in his exile at Bologna. He vividly communicates the sense of the artist wandering about the rather ugly streets and coming upon Jacopo's sculpture almost by chance.

> Bologna, with its endless colonnades and fantastic leaning towers, has never been one of the lovelier cities of Italy. But about the portals of its vast unfinished churches and dark shrines, half-hidden by votive flowers and candles, lie some of the sweetest works of the early Tuscan sculptors, Giovanni da Pisa and Jacopo della Quercia, things soft as flowers; and the year which Michelangelo spent in copying these works was not a lost year.[49]

Ruskin had nothing to say about Michelangelo's debt to the sculpture of the fifteenth century, but he did see similarities between Michelangelo and the work of the ancient Greeks. Michelangelo, he says, cannot rival the Greeks, but he is like them in that he concentrates on mere physique at the expense of facial expression. He says they both "delight in the body for its own sake, and cast it into every conceivable attitude, often in violation of all natural probability,"[50] and both, Ruskin claims, ignore the expressive potential of the face. Now this comparison between the classic work of Greece, which, of course Michelangelo never knew, and the depiction of the nude in his work had often been made – usually to the detriment of Michelangelo. For example, only a few months before Ruskin delivered his lecture in Oxford, the Slade Professor at Cambridge, Digby Wyatt, had written: "Powerful and grand as unquestionably are the immortal monuments of the Medici at Florence, and the Moses at Rome, there is yet a certain uncouthness in their rendering which leaves them far beneath the best figures of Grecian art."[51] Wyatt's use of the word "uncouth," and Ruskin's accusations of Michelangelo's posturing have their origins in the view promulgated by Winckelmann that Michelangelo "debauched the artists from Grace"; he "disdained to stoop to tender feelings and lovely grace ... Immoderately fond of all that was extraordinary and difficult, he ... broke through the bounds of antiquity, grace and nature; and as he painted for occasions of displaying skill only, he grew extravagant."[52] The idea that Michelangelo violated the standards of perfection established in ancient Greece was spread in Germany by Raphael Mengs, in Italy by Francesco Milizia, and in France by Étienne Falconet. "If you place one or two antique pieces of the same kind beside the Bacchus of Michelangelo," said Falconet, "you would immediately see the difference."[53] In this country Tobias Smollett seems to have read his Winckelmann before travelling to Italy. "Michael Angelo," he writes, "with all his skill in anatomy, his correctness of design ... and force of expression, seems to have very little idea of grace."[54] Like many writers after him he missed the calm serenity of the antique in Michelangelo's *Last Judgement*, seeing it as "a mere mob, without subordination, keeping or repose."[55] Shelley, too, felt that Michelangelo violated aesthetic propriety in the Sistine Chapel. When he visited Naples in 1819 he had just been reading a French translation of Winckelmann, and on seeing a study by Michelangelo for the *Last Judgement* said: "I cannot but think the genius of this artist highly overrated. He has not only no temperance no modesty no feeling for the just boundaries of art ... but he has no sense of beauty, and to want this is to want the essence of the creative power of mind."[56] The controversy about the authenticity of the Elgin marbles and the cult which grew up around them did nothing to enhance the reputation of Michelangelo. Hazlitt, for example, who had been deeply moved by Lord Elgin's treasures reported that the Sistine Chapel was "like an immense field of battle, or a charnel-house, strewed with carcasses and naked bodies ... a shambles of Art," and Benjamin Robert Haydon compared Michelangelo's sculpture with that of the Elgin marbles in his journal of 1814. He wrote:

> I am convinced from what I see, that Michel [sic] Angelo had no permanent principle of form. He could not extricate the superfluous from the accidental, he burthened his figures with ostentatious anatomy, with useless and subordinate parts.
> Michel Angelo's forms have no refinement; they are heavy, not grand; they are the forms of porters and mechanics. The Theseus of the Elgin Marbles is really grand, and you can see that the gladiator's form is not the product of labour, but the harmonious combination of subtle nature. He is a refined gentleman, a prince, handsome and educated. Michel Angelo would have made him fierce, turbulent, vulgar, more bulky but not so sublime.[57]

Similarly Charles Dickens, some years later, was unable to discern "any general idea, or one pervading thought, in harmony with the stupendous subject."[58] In the nineteenth century there were two answers to this neoclassical hostility to Michelangelo. One was what might be called ontological, the other was stylistic. The ontological argument was adopted by

Stendhal, A.F. Rio,[59] and Michael Scott and ran something like this: the art of ancient Greece and the art of Michelangelo are different in kind. The first was the product of a pagan cosmology, the second of a Christian one. Since the fifth century BC, man's attitude to himself and his relationship with his gods had changed in a profound way. The sense of ease in the world and the spiritual self-confidence had been replaced by the conviction of sin, damnation and redemption. Consequently it was foolish to look for equanimity in either the *Last Judgement* or the sculpture of Michelangelo since they expressed the modern not the ancient sensibility. Pater is aware of this argument but does not press it in his essay. He points out that the Adam of the Sistine Chapel is as "fair as the young men of the Elgin marbles" but quite "unlike them in a total absence of that balance and completeness which expresses so well the sentiment of a self-contained, independent life."[60] But Pater says nothing about the religious issues. Instead, he adopts an interesting stylistic thesis which he almost certainly derived from J.C. Robinson's catalogue of the 1862 South Kensington Exhibition. In his preliminary notice to the sculpture of the fifteenth and sixteenth centuries Robinson wrote: "The world has seen two great and distinct systems of sculpture; that of the ancient Greeks, the crowning glory of which were the Parthenon sculptures of Phidias, and the very different but perhaps not less admirable art of modern Italy in the 15th and 16th centuries; the works of Michael Angelo, in the cities of Florence and Rome, being unquestionably to this latter time what those of the great sculptor of Athens were to all other ancient art."[61] In his essay on Lucca della Robbia, written shortly after the Michelangelo piece, Pater describes the history of sculpture in identical terms, as what he calls "the system of the Greek sculptors and the system of Michelangelo,"[62] and he goes on to make a contrast between the works of Michelangelo which is very similar to that of Robinson's. Michelangelo's art, said Robinson, "was widely different from that of Phidias, different indeed from all antique art, and in nothing more than in its intense personality; ancient art was an all-pervading system, absorbing and levelling in its sublime abstraction all individualities; everything in it was expressed literally, materially, but it had little inward or subjective expression, and in this the art of Michael Angelo was supreme ... his impersonations live with an intense vitality, a passionate earnestness and fulness of meaning pervade them all."[63] Similarly, Pater contrasts the "breadth, generality, universality" of classical art with the intense expressiveness of Michelangelo's work. The first, he says, "purges from the individual all that belongs only to him, all the accidents, the feelings, and actions of a special moment,"[64] whereas Michelangelo "came ... with a genius spiritualised by the reverie of the middle age, penetrated by its spirit of inwardness and introspection, living not a mere outward life like the Greek, but a life full of inward experiences, sorrows, consolations."[65] Pater develops Robinson's idea of the "intense vitality" in Michelangelo's work by concentrating on those moments of becoming, of birth and of nascent life that he depicts. The "Resurrection is the real subject of his last work in the Sistine" says Pater.

Adam's "whole form is gathered into an expression of mere expectation and reception."[67] Michelangelo's favourite Pagan subject is the legend of Leda, the delight of the world breaking from the egg of a bird.[68] The means by which Michelangelo achieves what Pater calls this "penetrative suggestion of life" is through his "studied incompleteness." "His persons," says Pater, "have something of the unwrought stone about them, so, as if to realise the expression by which the old Florentine records describe a sculptor – *master of live stone* – with him the very rocks seem to have life. They have but to cast away the dust and scurf that they may rise and stand on their feet."[69]

Though many writers mention the incompleteness of Michelangelo's sculpture, few authors in the nineteenth century use it to explain the potent sense of life he communicates. This idea owes little to J. C. Robinson but it does have striking affinities with the work of two men whose accounts of Michelangelo Pater certainly knew. The first is the late eighteenth-century historian of art Seroux d'Agincourt; the other strangely enough is Ruskin himself.

In his appreciation of Michelangelo in the second volume of *L'Histoire de l'art par les monumens* (1823) Seroux d'Agincourt selected for special praise Michelangelo's ability to capture the transient movements of the body. Like Pater after him, d'Agincourt detected a sense of creative vitality in both the sculpture and the painting. He wrote: "If Michelangelo is admirable for mastering [in paint] the subtle and passing effects of life in the human body, he is even greater for making it felt in certain ways in his statuary; one can see movement and action born in them." He continued, "This is particularly true of the incomplete pieces or in parts of those which he had just rough-hewn. There one can see clearly the stages by which he induced into his work the feeling of vitality." D'Agincourt's conclusion also very closely resembles one of the dominant themes of Pater's essay. "Through this rare man," he wrote, "we are made spectators of a kind of creation."[70] We know that Pater had read d'Agincourt,[71] he had also read Ruskin, who, twenty-five years before his lecture on "Michael Angelo and Tintoret," had claimed that Michelangelo's was "the greatest mind that art ever inspired."[72] In the second volume of *Modern Painters* in the chapter "Imagination Penetrative" Ruskin anticipates Pater in a number of ways. Like Pater, Ruskin interprets the "tenderness" of Michelangelo in terms of his predecessors in the fifteenth century. Michelangelo, he says, goes beyond the "intense truth, tenderness, and power of men like Mino da Fiesole,"[73] and in the figure of Adam in the Sistine Chapel he recreates the feeling of nascent vitality. For Pater, Adam embodies the idea of the "expectation and reception" of life; and Ruskin uses a series of verbs which also suggest the anticipation of life. He speaks of "the earth of the Sistine Adam that begins to burn ... the twelve great torrents of the Spirit of God that pauses above us there ... waiting in the shadow of Futurity ... each ... fixed in his expectation, silent forseeing."[74] For Pater to use an idea from Ruskin's youthful appreciation of Michelangelo so soon after the Slade lecture seems like a wry but subtle comment on Ruskin's profound change of mind about the artist.

Finally, of the many differences in their approach to Michelangelo none is more striking than the way in which Pater and Ruskin treat the biographical details – the personal life of Michelangelo and his inner struggle. For Ruskin, Michelangelo's work offers no personal feeling or human expression, so, naturally, the biography is of no interest to him. In complete contrast, Pater devotes a large proportion of his essay to what he calls the legend of Michelangelo and treats the poetry as the clearest evidence of the gentle melancholy in the artist's nature. Once again Ruskin's view conforms with an older, received idea of Michelangelo. Turning to Winckelmann we find that Michelangelo was "a pure intelligence" which "despised all that could please humanity."[75] Even Reynolds spoke of his lack of concern with anything commonplace, and of the "superior order of beings" that populated his pictures;[76] Hazlitt suggested that in his art "all is in lofty repose and solitary grandeur, which no human interest can shake or disturb";[77] Fuseli pointed out how "the child, the female, meanness, deformity were by him indiscriminately stamped with grandeur."[78] In France, Stendhal bemoaned the absence of unaffected simple emotion in his work,[79] and Baudelaire compared the statues in the Medici Chapel with Titans.[80] A contemporary of Pater, however, summed up a change which had recently come over Michelangelo criticism. Writing in 1870 Bernard Woodward said that previously people had thought of Michelangelo as "colossal, solitary [and] cold." Now, however, he wrote:

> The means of affording a truer judgment have been made more widely known. Less has been thought of the daring individuality of his manner, and more weight has been given to those touches of nature which are seen in his works, and which claim kindred with the world.[81]

The "means of affording" this "truer judgement" of Michelangelo came mainly from two important publications in the early years of the 1860s. The first was a substantial biographical study by the German Hermann Grimm which came out in 1860-3, and the second was the publication of the first authentic text of Michelangelo's *Rime* by Cesare Guasti in 1863.[82] Pater quotes freely from Grimm and he is the first writer in English to make substantial use of what John Addington Symonds called the "laborious and minute scholarship" of Guasti.[83] Previous biographies of Michelangelo depended heavily on the account of the artist's life in Vasari's *Lives of the Painters* supplemented by a more intimate account written by Michelangelo's friend Condivi.[84] Grimm used a mass of previously unpublished archival material to give a far more accurate and detailed account of the day to day life of Michelangelo and his relations with various Papal patrons. As for the *Rime* all the translations and the literary critical judgements had previously been based on an extremely corrupt text published in 1623 by Michelangelo's great-nephew. This was so expurgated and so made to conform with current literary practice that it was no more than a pale shadow of the original verses. Until the original manuscripts were made available to Guasti by the Buonarroti family these *rifacimenti*, as they came to be known, were accepted as the authentic work of the artist. Guasti's work dispelled the maudlin and sentimental tradition that had grown up around Michelangelo and Vittoria Colonna,[85] and Pater accepts Guasti's view that many of the sonnets were addressed not to Vittoria, but to one or more young men. Finally, however, Pater evaded the question of Michelangelo's homosexuality and it was left to John Addington Symonds in his 1877 translation of the sonnets to put what he called the "literal interpretation" on them.[86]

Pater may well have chosen to concentrate on the poetry of Michelangelo in his essay because it throws into relief aspects of the artist's character which found almost no direct expression in the painting and sculpture. Ruskin chose to overlook the contemplative, sensitive and religious aspects of Michelangelo which would have detracted from his argument, but Pater was not the first to feel that to understand Michelangelo one had to understand his poetry. Edgar Quinet, for example, in a book which Pater knew well, clearly stated that "the record of the struggles of this great soul is to be found in the poetry ... it is the confessional revelation in which the torments of this spirit torn between the two tendencies of his age are revealed with a lucid clarity,"[87] and though Pater may have taken from Quinet the hint about the importance of the poetry, one aspect of Pater's treatment of Michelangelo is extremely unusual. It is concerned with the word "sweetness" which Pater uses in this essay some nineteen times. The "true type of the Michelangelesque," he says, is "sweetness and strength"; the "penetrative suggestion of life" is the key to "the secret of that sweetness"; Michelangelo yearns to be "sweet and pensive" as Dante; the prevailing tone of the sonnets is "a strange interfusion of sweetness and strength," and so on.[88] Now the feminine quality of "sweetness" is used very rarely in critical accounts of Michelangelo. The masculine attributes of "strength," "power" and "sublimity" are repeated many times and in many languages but the word "sweetness" is almost never used.[89] There is one passage in one book, however, in which it is used and this passage is interesting in the context of Pater's essay for a number of reasons. Not only is it an outright attack on Winckelmann's attitude to Michelangelo; it also anticipates Pater's emphasis on the sensitive, restrained and tentative qualities in Michelangelo's art. The passage occurs in an edition of Winckelmann's *Werke* which Pater had used some years before when he was writing his essay on the German critic. The edition was published in Dresden in 1826 with extensive notes by Johann Heinrich Meyer.[90] Rather in the way in which Pater must have felt that Ruskin had been unfair to Michelangelo, so Meyer felt that Winckelmann had overlooked an important aspect of Michelangelo's genius. "To some of our readers," says Meyer, "Winckelmann's view of Michelangelo and Bernini may seem hard and even unjust,"[91] and he invites those same readers to consider another aspect of Michelangelo's work. He suggests that they turn from the images of power and strength that have preoccupied people for so long and consider the Michelangelo of the *Rime*. There they will find gentleness, mildness, and what is particularly significant, a feminine side to what appears to be a deeply masculine nature. In Meyer's words:

> In these rare poems, until recently little known abroad, the great Michelangelo reveals himself in a way which will surprise and amaze all those who know him only through his pictures and statues. The underlying tone of this warm and passionate poetry is a sincere admiration for true beauty, a deep but unrequited love, a sweet [sanft] and touching melancholy for a vision which is not satisfied in its desire for infinite love ... in this poetry Michelangelo has given expression to the feminine aspects of his great and powerful nature in a way which is all the more lovely for the fact that the masculine principle is dominant in his other works of art.[92]

When Pater came to write about Michelangelo in 1871 it would have been quite natural for him to turn to this famous passage in Winckelmann about Michelangelo and Bernini. If he were about to write an oblique response to Ruskin's diatribe (about which incidentally Ruskin himself remained impenitent),[93] then Meyer would have provided him with one possible strategy. But can we be sure that Pater heard Ruskin? One final piece of evidence suggests that he did. It is connected with the *Nouvelle Biographie Générale* kept in the library of Brasenose College. When he was writing the essays for *The Renaissance* Pater often used this biographical dictionary with its lengthy entries and its copious bibliography. It was a useful way of gathering general information about historical characters and material for further research. On 18 June 1871, five days after Ruskin's lecture, Pater borrowed volume 35-6[94] and it is no coincidence that it is this volume that contains the substantial entry for "Michelangelo Buonarroti."

J. B. BULLEN
University of Reading

NOTES

1. John Ruskin, "The Relation between Michael Angelo and Tintoret. Seventh of the course of lectures on sculpture delivered at Oxford, 1870-71," in *The Works of John Ruskin*, ed. E. T. Cook and Alexander Wedderburn (London: George Allen, 1906). XXII, 83.
2. Ruskin, *Works*, XXII, 87.
3. *Fortnightly Review*, NS 10 (Nov. 1871), 559-70.
4. "Twenty-Three Sonnets from Michael Angelo," *Contemporary Review*, 20 (1872), 506.
5. In June 1871 Pater borrowed books from the libraries of Brasenose College and the Taylor Institution, Oxford. For this information I am indebted to Billie Andrew Inman's "Walter Pater's Borrowings from the Queen's College Library, the Bodleian

Library, the Brasenose College Library, and the Taylor Institution Library, 1860-1894," unpublished typescript (1977). See also note 94.

6. Edward Poynter, "Professor Ruskin on Michelangelo," in *Ten Lectures on Art* (London, 1879), p.219. In the same month as Ruskin's lecture Poynter published an appreciative account of Michelangelo's work in which he commented: "I have heard it said again and again, by artists (who ought to know better) and others, that Michelangelo's works may be grand in style, they may be imaginative, they may even be beautiful (sometimes), but they cannot be said to be true to Nature on account of their exaggeration. You will recognise that this is a common way in which Michelangelo's works are spoken of." "Beauty and Realism," *Fortnightly Review*, NS 9 (June 1871), 726. Poynter's remark suggests that there was in existence considerable hostility to Michelangelo.

7. Ruskin, *Works*, XXII, xxxi.

8. G[eorgina] B[urne]-J[ones], *Memorials of Edward Burne-Jones* (London: Macmillan, 1904), II, 18.

9. Ruskin, *Works*, XXII, 79.

10. Walter Pater, *The Renaissance. Studies in Art and Poetry*, ed. Donald L. Hill (Berkeley, Los Angeles, London: California U.P., 1980), p.76.

11. Ruskin, *Works*, XXII, 85.

12. Carlo Cesare Malvasia, *Vite de pittori bolognesi ... etc.*, 2 vols. (Bologna, 1678) and Giovanni Pietro Bellori, *Le Vite de' pittori, scultori et architetti moderni* (Rome, 1672).

13. F. Scanelli, *Il microcosmo della pittura* (Cesena, 1657) and G.P. Lomazzo, *Tempio della pittura* (Venice, 1590).

14. Giorgio Melchiori in *Michelangelo nel settecento inglese* (Rome: Edizioni di Storia e Letteratura, 1950), 46-7 gives an extract from Rosa's Third Satire entitled *La pittura* with the translation:

> Good Michael Angelo, I do not Jest,
> Thy pencil a Great Judgment hath exprest;
> But in that Judgment thou, alas, hast shown
> A very little Judgment of Thy own!

15. Roland Fréart, "To the Reader," in *An Idea of Perfection in Painting*, trans. John Evelyn (London, 1668).

16. Jonathan Richardson, *An Account of Some of the Statues, Bas Reliefs, Drawings and Pictures in Italy with Remarks* (London, 1722), p.270.

17. *History of Ancient Art* (1764) in *Winckelmann, Writings on Art* ed. David Irwin (London: Phaidon, 1972), p.118.

18. An account of Michelangelo and the sublime can be found in Melchiori, *Michelangelo nel settecento inglese*, pp.33 ff.

19. Joshua Reynolds, *Discourses on Art*, ed. Robert R. Wark (Berkeley, Los Angeles, London: California U.P., 1969), p.282.

20. *Lectures on Painting by Royal Academicians, Barry, Opie and Fuseli*, ed. Ralph N. Wornum (London, 1848), p.466.

21. See O.E.D.

22. John Courtney, *The Present State of the Manners, Arts and Politics of France and Italy* (London, 1794). Quoted Melchiori, p.71. Set against this English enthusiasm for Michelangelo is the contempt felt for him on the continent. This culminated in Francesco Milizia's *Dell'arte di vedere nelle belle arti* (1781) which claimed that "in all the painted and sculpted works of Michelangelo he makes such a display of his anatomical knowledge that he seems to have worked solely for the sake of anatomy, and unfortunately he neither understood it nor applied it correctly" (pp.16-17). Charles Eastlake explained some of this hostility as a belated reaction to Vasari. See *Contributions to the Literature of the Fine Arts*, Second Series (London, 1870), pp.276-7.

23. Ruskin, *Works*, XXII, 81.

24. Pater, *The Renaissance*, p.57.

25. Pater, *The Renaissance*, p.57.

26. *The Works of Jonathan Richardson* (London, 1792), p.97.

27. *Lectures ... by Royal Academicians*, p. 382. Matthew Pilkington, *The Gentleman's and Connoisseur's Dictionary of Painters* of 1770 says of Michelangelo: "His attitudes are not always beautiful, or pleasing; and he was (as Fresnoy observes) bold, even to rashness, in which he often succeeded. His works always surprise the beholder, with the appearance of somewhat unusually great, though they may not always afford pleasure" (p. 11).

28. Reynolds, *Discourses*, p. 83.

29. *Aretin, or a Dialogue on Painting*, trans. William Brown (London, 1770), p. 28.

30. Wordsworth (see note 31) may have seen this idea in Dolce, too. Dolce wrote: "As Homer ranks first among the Greeks, Virgil among the Romans, and Dante among the Italian poets, so does Michael Angelo among painters and sculptors of the present age" (*Aretin*, p. 28). In his *Memoirs of Painting* (1824) William Buchanan expressed similar views. Michelangelo, he said, "was the Homer of Epic Painting" (I, 30). See also Fuseli: "[Michelangelo] is the inventor of epic painting." *Lectures ... by Royal Academicians*, p. 382.

31. *The Life and Letters of William Bewick*, ed. Thomas Landseer (London, 1871), I, 87-8. These remarks were made to Benjamin Robert Haydon and the famous exiled Italian poet Ugo Foscolo in Haydon's house, Lisson Grove. (See E. R. Vincent, *Ugo Foscolo: An Italian in Regency England* [Cambridge: Cambridge U.P., 1953], p. 14.) Foscolo had written two articles on the poetry of Michelangelo, one in the *New Monthly Magazine*, IV (1882), 339 and one in the *Retrospective Review*, XIII (1826), 248. Sir Thomas Lawrence, who was the English collector of the Michelangelo drawings in the Ashmolean Museum, Oxford, decided to signal his election as President of the Royal Academy by presenting to the Academy School a series of full-sized copies in oil of Michelangelo's Prophets and Sibyls from the Sistine Chapel. According to Landseer it was Foscolo who was the first to suggest that Bewick might be employed on the task. Accordingly, Bewick left for Rome in 1826 and was paid one hundred guineas for a copy of the Delphic Sibyl (See Bewick, II, 74 and 273).

32. Michael Scott, "On Michael Angelo's Last Judgment," *Blackwood's Edinburgh Magazine*, 45 (Jan.-June 1839), 266.

33. Scott, p. 257.

34. Lindsay, *Sketches of the History of Christian Art*, 2nd. ed. (London, 1885), II, 215.

35. Stendhal, *Histoire de la peinture en Italie* (1817) new ed. (Paris, 1868), p. 368: Delacroix, "Sur le Jugement Dernier," *Revue des Deux Mondes*, 4ième série, 11 (Aug. 1837), 337-44: Baudelaire, "L'Idéal," in *Les Fleurs du Mal*, ed. Antoine Adam (Paris: Garnier, 1961), p. 25: Quinet, *Les Révolutions d'Italie* (1848) in *Oeuvres Complètes* (Paris, 1857), IV, 363-75: Michelet, *La Renaissance* (Paris, 1885), pp. 226-42: Taine, *Voyage en Italie* (Paris, 1866), I, 277. It seems likely that Swinburne's fevered account of some Michelangelo drawings in the Uffizi owes something to this French tradition. He wrote: "Not gratitude, not delight, not sympathy, is the first sense excited in one suddenly confronted with his [i.e. Michelangelo's] designs; fear rather, oppressive reverence and well nigh intolerable adoration" ("Notes on Designs of the Old Masters at Florence" [1868] in *The Complete Works of Algernon Charles Swinburne*, ed. Sir E. Gosse and R. J. Wise [London and New York: Heinemann, 1926], V, 157).

36. Delacroix, "Michel-Ange," (1830) in *Oeuvres Littéraires* (Paris: G. Crès, 1923), II, 33.

37. Michelet, *La Renaissance*, p. 231: Taine, *Voyage*, I, 282.

38. Ruskin, *Works*, XXII, 87.

39. Ruskin, *Works*, XXII, 100.

40. Pater, *The Renaissance*, p. 71. Pater probably had Alfred Dumesnil in mind. Dumesnil wrote that Michelangelo "nous montrerait ces travailleurs solitaires du passé, revenant, dans leurs fils plus libres." *L'Art italien* (Paris, 1854), p. 220.

41. Pater, *The Renaissance*, p. 71. It is conceivable that Pater was going to strengthen the connections between Michelangelo and early art in an essay which now exists only in a MS copy. His "Arezzo" or "Prelude to Michelangelo" (Harvard University: Literary and Scholarly Papers, b. MS Eng., 1150) was written, Laurel Brake suggests, in August 1872. Pater may have later decided against including it in *The Renaissance*. See Laurel Brake, "A Commentary on 'Arezzo': An Unpublished Manuscript by Walter Pater,"

Review of English Studies, NS 27 (Aug. 1976), 266-76.

42. Pater, *The Renaissance*, p. 52.
43. John Addington Symonds published a substantial account of Michelangelo's debt to Signorelli in "Orvieto," *The Cornhill Magazine*, 11 (Jan.-June 1865), 164.
44. Flaxman, "Modern Sculpture" (1826) in *Lectures on Sculpture*, new ed. (London, 1865), p. 252.
45. A. C. Quatremère de Quincy, *Histoire de la vie et des ouvrages de Michel-Ange Buonarroti* (Paris, 1835).
46. Leopold Cicognara wrote that "at that time Michelangelo did not find the arts in a state of infancy, but developed, mature and powerful in all their various aspects," and of the way in which previous writers had treated Michelangelo's forebears he said: "They spoke of the arts before his time with disrespect and unpardonable ingratitude" (*Storia della scultura dal suo risorgimento in Italia ... etc.* [Venice, 1813], V, 225 [my translation]). Gustave Garrison commented that "M. Quatremère de Quincy s'écrie que Michel-Ange fut le véritable révélateur de l'art, qu'il n'eut de maîtres en aucun genre, qu'il créa à la fois la science du dessin et sculpture moderne" (*Michel-Ange et son temps* [Toulouse, 1859], p. 10).
47. Robinson, *Italian Sculpture of the Middle Ages and Period of the Revival of Art* (London, 1862), p. 130.
48. Perkins, *Tuscan Sculptors, Their Lives, Works and Times* (London, 1864), I, 109-10.
49. Pater, *The Renaissance*, p. 62.
50. Ruskin, *Works*, XXII, 95.
51. Wyatt, *Fine Art ... Being a Course of Lectures Delivered at Cambridge in 1870* (London and New York, 1870), p. 139.
52. Winckelmann, *Reflections on the Painting and Sculpture of the Greeks ... etc.*, trans. H. Fuseli (London, 1765), p. 283 and p. 284.
53. Falconet wrote: "Cependant le *Bacchus* de *Michel-Ange* est une statue manierée, d'une étude fausse, les chairs en sont rondes ... le dessein incorrect dans presque toutes les parties. ... Si [on] mettoit à côté d'elle deux ou trois belles statues antiques du même caratere [sic] on seroit étonné de la difference" (*Oeuvres d'Étienne Falconet* [Lausanne, 1791], I, 338). Du Fresnoy and De Piles were often cited as authorities for Michelangelo's unclassical awkwardness. For example in Dryden's translation Du Fresnoy says: "The choice which he made of his Postures was not always beautiful or pleasing; His Gift of Designing was not the finest, nor his Outlines the most elegant ... He was not a little fantastical and extravagant in his Compositions" (*The Art of Painting*, trans. J. Dryden [London, 1695], p. 214); and de Piles corroborates this view. "His *Attitudes* are for the most part disagreeable, the *Airs* of his *Heads* fierce, his *Draperies* not open enough, and his *Expressions* not very natural" (*The Art of Painting and the Lives of the Painters*, trans. anon. [London, 1706], p. 161). This attitude reached its apogee in the writings of Francesco Milizia. He said that, "In tutte le opere scolpite e dipinte, Michelangelo fa pompe sì grande della sua scienza anatomica: e per disgrazia egli non l'ha nè bene applicata" (*Dell' arte di vedere ... etc.* [Venice, 1798], pp. 16-17).
54. Smollett, *Travels Through France and Italy* (London, 1766), II, 127.
55. Smollett, *Travels*, II, 126.
56. *The Letters of Percy Bysshe Shelley*, ed. Frederick L. Jones (Oxford U.P., 1964), II, 80.
57. *The Complete Works of William Hazlitt*, ed. P. P. Howe (London and Toronto: Dent, 1930-4), XVII, 144, and *Life of Benjamin Robert Haydon* ed. Tom Taylor (London, 1853), I, 214-15. Haydon changed his mind about Michelangelo, for in 1810 he wrote to Sir George Beaumont that "such fame as Ananias gained for Raffaele, and the Capella Sistina for Michel Angelo, [sic] is, and ever shall be, my object" (*Life*, I, 130).
58. Dickens, *Pictures From Italy*, 2nd. ed. (London 1846), p. 209. Curiously Elizabeth Barrett Barrett attributed the popularity of Dickens's *Pictures From Italy* (which she confuses with the *Cricket on the Hearth*) to his disparaging remarks about Michelangelo. She pointed out to her future husband, Robert Browning, that "it sells by nineteen thousand copies at a time, though he takes Michael Angelo to be a 'humbug' — or for 'though' read 'because'." (Letter dated 21 December 1845 in *The Letters of Robert Browning and Elizabeth Barrett Barrett 1845-1846*, ed. Elvan Kintner [Cam-

bridge Mass.: Harvard U.P., 1969], I, 342.) Elizabeth Barrett had, like Ruskin, been brought up on Rogers' poem *Italy* (1836) with the famous lines on the Medici Tomb (pp. 104-5) and which Ruskin described as "the only instance ... of just and entire appreciation of Michael Angelo's spiritual power" (Ruskin, *Works*, IV, 282, note). Rogers had in his possession a "small model, by Michael Angelo, of his famous statue of Lorenzo de' Medici, Duke of Urbino," according to Anna Jameson (*Companion to the Most Celebrated Private Galleries of Art in London* [London, 1844], p. 411), and when Elizabeth Barrett went to see the collection in 1846 she wrote about "a statuette in clay, alive with the life of Michael Angelo's finger – the blind eyes looking ... seeing ... as if in scorn of all clay" (*Letters*, ed. Kintner, II, 806). Consequently she gave the work of Michelangelo pride of place in *Casa Guidi Windows* (1851: 11.73-144).

59. A.F. Rio in *Michel-Ange et Raphael* (Paris, 1867).
60. Pater, *The Renaissance*, p. 59.
61. Robinson, *Italian Sculpture*, p. 129.
62. Pater, *The Renaissance*, p. 53.
63. Robinson, *Italian Sculpture*, p. 130.
64. Pater, *The Renaissance*, p. 51.
65. Pater, *The Renaissance*, p. 52 (text of 1873).
66. Pater, *The Renaissance*, p. 59.
67. Pater, *The Renaissance*, p. 59 (text of 1871).
68. Pater, *The Renaissance*, p. 59.
69. Pater, *The Renaissance*, pp. 59-60.
70. D'Agincourt wrote: "Si Michel-Ange est admirable pour avoir su rendre avec cette vérité la vie fuyant du corps humain, il est encore bien plus pour l'avoir fait sentir arrivant en quelque sorte dans les statues qu'animait son ciseau; on y voit naître le mouvement et l'action. C'est particulièrement dans les figures qu'il a laissées impar-faites, ou dans quelques parties de celles qu'il a simplement ébauchées, qu'on apperçoit clairement la gradation avec la quelle il faisait entrer le sentiment vital dans ses ouvrages. ... Cet homme rare rend ainsi présens à une espèce de creation" (*Histoire de l'art par les monumens* [Paris, 1823], II, 88).
71. B.A. Inman points out in the essay referred to above that Pater borrowed Seroux d'Agincourt from the Bodleian Library on 9 October, 1866.
72. Ruskin, *Modern Painters II* (1846) in *Works* IV, 280.
73. Ruskin, *Works*, IV, 281.
74. Ruskin, *Works*, IV, 281. Ruskin's attitude to Michelangelo in 1846 is closely allied with the 'superman' tradition developed in France. Rather like Taine a little later, Ruskin linked the names of Michelangelo, Phidias and Dante as "three colossal images standing up side by side, looming in their great rest of spirituality above the whole world-horizon" (*Works*, IV, 118). Ruskin pleads that his earlier attitude to Michelangelo was merely the conventional attitude of the 1840s, but B.A. Inman argues cogently for a different explanation. She claims that Ruskin's later hostility is more consistent with his general assessment of the evil nature of the Italian Renaissance, and that his change of mind was a process of rationalisation rather than a spontaneous aesthetic response (See Billie Andrew Inman, "Ruskin's Reasoned Criticism of Art," *Papers on Language and Literature*, 13 [1977], 372-82).
75. Winckelmann, *Reflections*, trans. Fuseli, p. 283.
76. Reynolds, *Discourses*, p. 83.
77. Hazlitt, "Fine Arts" (1817), in *Works*, ed. Howe, XVIII, 116.
78. Fuseli, *Lectures ... by Royal Academicians*, p. 540.
79. Stendhal, *Histoire de la Peinture*, p. 377.
80. In "L'Idéal" Baudelaire wrote:

> Ou bien toi, grande Nuit, fille de Michel-Ange,
> Qui tors paisiblement dans une pose étrange
> Tes appas façonnés aux bouches des Titans!

(*Les Fleurs du Mal* ed. Antoine Adam [Paris: Garnier, 1961], p. 25).

81. Woodward, *Specimens of the Drawings of Ten Masters from the Royal Collection at Windsor Castle* (London, 1870), p.22.
82. Grimm, *Das Leben Michelangelos*, 2 vols. (Hanover, 1860-3), and Guasti, *Le Rime di Michelangelo Buonarroti* (Florence, 1863).
83. Symonds, *The Sonnets of Michael Angelo Buonarroti* (1877), 3rd ed. (London: Smith, Elder, 1912), pp. xi-xii.
84. *Vita di Michelagnolo Buonarroti raccolta per Ascanio Condivi de La Ripa Transone* (Rome, 1553). There was a substantial amount of biographical material available to Pater. Richard Duppa's *The Life and Literary Works of Michel Angelo Buonarroti* (London, 1806) contains the biography together with translations of the poetry by Wordsworth and Southey with whom Duppa was friendly. It also contains extensive illustrative material of the sculpture, painting and architecture. It was popularised by publication in Bogue's "European Library" in 1846 and Bohn's competing "Standard Library" in 1849. A. C. Quatremère de Quincy's *Histoire de la vie ... de Michel-Ange Buonarroti* (Paris, 1835) has already been mentioned. As permanent secretary of the Academy of Fine Art and art editor of the *Journal des Savants* de Quincy was very influential. More original, however, was John S. Harford's *The Life of Michael Angelo Buonarroti* 2 vols. (London, 1857) because Harford attempted to relate Michelangelo's work to the intellectual and philosophical life of Renaissance Italy. Together with Grimm, we know that Pater used Charles Clément's *Michel-Ange, Léonard de Vinci, Raphael ... etc.* Inman, "Borrowings," reports that Pater borrowed it from the Taylor Institution Library between 27 May and 15 June 1868. It contains a well-written, if slight exposition of Michelangelo's life and work which was highly popular. It reached its fifth edition in 1881, was translated into English by Louisa Corkran in 1880, and the essay on Michelangelo was published separately in 1880. Grimm's *Michelangelo* advanced the tendency of all these biographies to relate the work of Michelangelo to other aspects of Renaissance culture. Grimm's attempt was much more adventurous than previous books, but it was marred by a Teutonic desire to be all-inclusive. Considerably revised in 1875 and translated into English by F. E. Bunnètt in 1865 it was for a long time the standard biography of Michelangelo.
85. Maria Roscoe in her *Vittoria Colonna: Her Life and Poems* (London, 1868) sums up a long tradition of the sentimental relations between Michelangelo and Vittoria. See also Cicognara, *Storia della scultura* (1813), V, 175; William Roscoe, *Life of Lorenzo de' Medici* (1797) new ed. (London, 1846), p.89; Harford, *The Life of Michael Angelo* (1857), I, 34-71; "Poems of Michel Angelo Buonarroti," *Retrospective Review*, 13 (1826), 264; John Edward Taylor, *Michelangelo Considered as a Philosophical Poet* (London, 1840), p.67; and D. G. Rossetti, "Michelangelo's Kiss," in *The House of Life* (London, 1870).
86. Symonds, *Renaissance in Italy: The Fine Arts* (London, 1877), p.521.
87. Quinet wrote: L'histoire des révolutions de ce grand esprit est dans les poésies qu'il a laissées. Ce sont les confessions où se révèlent, avec une clarté ingénue, les tourmentes de cette âme partagée entre les deux tendances de son siècle" (*Les Révolutions d'Italie* [1848] in *Oeuvres Complètes* [Paris, 1857], IV, 363-4, borrowed by Pater from the Taylor Institute Library on 17 Dec. 1864. See Inman, "Borrowings." Quinet's treatment of Michelangelo as the reconciler of Christian and Pagan forces at work in the Renaissance [qui associent Platon et Moise, Orphée et Jesus-Christ] closely resembles Pater's treatment of Michelangelo's *Tondo Doni* in the essay on Pico della Mirandola [*Renaissance*, p.37]).
88. Pater, *The Renaissance*, pp.57, 60, 64, 76.
89. As Professor B. A. Inman has pointed out to me, Swinburne had attributed "strength and sweetness" to both Hugo and Blake in "A Study of *Les Misérables* Part IV," *The Spectator* 26 July 1862, p.831, and in "Notes on Designs" he describes Blake as Michelangelo's "great disciple."
90. He borrowed the volume which is central to this argument from the Library of the Taylorian Institution between 19 April and 2 June 1866 (See Inman, "Borrowings").
91. Winckelmann, *Geschichte der Kunst der Altertums*, in *Werke*, ed. E.L. Fernow, Heinrich Meyer and Johann Schulze (Dresden, 1808-20), IV, 261. Meyer, though critical of Winckelmann, was brought up in Switzerland under his influence. In 1784 he went to

Italy where he met and deeply impressed Goethe. He later collaborated with Goethe in an attempt to acquaint the German public with all phases of art. Like Goethe he was a great admirer of Michelangelo and distrusted the new school of German religio-romanticism.

92. "In diesem seltnen und daher im Auslande wenig bekannten Gedichte offenbaret sich der grosse Michel Agnolo auf eine Weise, welche allen, die ihn nur aus seinen Gemälden und Statuen kennen, auffallend und wunderbar erscheinen muss. Innige Bewunderung wahrer Schönheiten, tiefe von ihrem Gegenstande nicht erhörte Liebe, sanfte rührende Wehmuth über die ganze Erscheinung des einer unendlichen Liebe nicht genügenden Lebens und eine hieraus sich erzeugende schwermüthige Sehnsucht nach Auflösung und Befreyung von den irdischen Fesseln, sind der Grundton dieser gluhendwarmen Gedichte, in welchen M. Agnolo das Weibliche seiner grossen gewaltigen Natur um so lieblicher ausspricht, je mehr in seinen übrigen Kunstwerken das männliche Princip überwiegend und hervortretend ist" (*Werke*, IV, 262).

93. On 27 May 1872 Ruskin wrote to Sir Henry Acland: "I am very glad I said what I did in my lecture on M. Angelo. The Sistine roof is one of the sorrowfullest pieces of affectation and abused power that have ever misled the world" (*Works*, XXII, xxvii).

94. *Nouvelle Biographie Général*, ed. M. Le d'Hoeffer, 46 vols. in 23 (Paris 1862).

A New Edition of Walter Pater's Collected Works:
A Forum

The following three brief essays by Sharon Bassett, Robert Seiler, and Hayden Ward are responses to an invitation by the editor to consider the nature of a new edition of Pater's works.

* * *

A Case for the Unretouched, if Imaginary, Portrait

While it is usually desirable – even required by the laws of editing – that authors be represented by the last text which there is good reason to believe they have seen through the presses, I would like to make a case that the proposed edition of the collected works of Walter Pater be an occasion on which we permit ourselves a reasoned waiver from the canons of editorial conservatism. I have come to feel about the 'book' publication of Pater's essays and lectures much as Pope's public must have felt when he published his letters – they leave out all the interesting parts.

Pater's place in the Victorian pantheon is always, to some extent at least, anomalous. Unlike most of his contemporaries who carefully modelled their lives on the *Bildungsroman* where the serenity of old age permitted the rationalized integration of youthful excesses, Pater seems to have developed backwards. While there is much recantation (to the relief of many of his supporters) there is an important sense in which the first formulation of a particular idea – when he was fresh from the stimulation of books and conversation – shows Pater most fully himself and most fully enacting his own critical mode. As the power of this stimulation waned, and as the essay was republished, Pater often spent the time during which the essay was being incorporated into books endeavouring to cover up his tracks. The textual history of many of the essays shows not so much the reversion to orthodoxy that is often alleged, as it does the loss of interest in the subject and a growing wish to be accepted by his contemporaries. The version of Pater that 'everyone' knows is as much a re-touched Imaginary Portrait as any Pater himself wrote. The Macmillan volumes on which the Collected Works was largely based are a fascinating and monumental version of Pater – the only version perhaps that he thought had any chance of surviving. But the version of Pater we find in those various blue or red volumes is not the Pater his contemporaries knew. The Pater of the 1870s and 1880s was assiduous in concealing the situational Pater of the 'sixties and early 'seventies. Since Pater was so elusive, reticent and inaccessible – note the lack of many crucial letters, journals (?), and MSS. – I believe that we are justified in bringing to light, in so far as we can, the Pater that struck terror in the hearts of dining companions at Oxford University. We would hardly know this figure of nineteenth-century Oxford if all we had to go on was the shadowy, mild, antiquarian figure portrayed by his book publications.

Bruce Vardon's 1950 dissertation – since superseded by Donald Hill's recent edition of *The Renaissance: Studies in Art and Poetry* – shows what I have called Pater's backward or reverse development. Vardon demonstrates with meticulous care the lengths to which Pater went, in the succeeding four editions of the Renaissance volume, to dismantle when possible, and to obscure when necessary, the enthusiasm of the young critic discovering the historicity of art and the imaginative presence of the past in every present. Vardon summarizes the changes Pater makes in the Winckelmann essay in the following way:

> Its numerous and important revisions fall in general into four categories: those in which Pater removes all traces of levity and boldness in speaking of the irreligious tendencies of Winckelmann; those in which he removes his attacks against Christianity as a whole, dogmatic and practical, and concentrates his attack instead on a narrow asceticism; those in which he weakens the force of statements inspired by his study of comparative religion and the 'higher criticism' of the Bible; finally, those in which he removes his disrespectful treatment of Roman Catholicism.[1]

Vardon makes the traditional assumption that the last version of the Winckelmann essay is nearer to what Pater 'really thought' – that Pater had finally seen clearly what had before been foggy and confused. And yet this version of the textual history of *Studies in the History of the Renaissance* fails to take into consideration the extent to which the original version of the Winckelmann essay fits into the development of what we understand to be Paterian aesthetic theory. It was after all published originally as a review article in *The Westminster Review*, and a few months earlier Pater had published two other crucial 'review essays' – "Coleridge's Writing" and "Poems by William Morris."

The original Winckelmann essay then bridges the worlds of the old and the new Romanticism, and begins that central argument in Pater's work that traces out the ways in which the Romantic movement is, in fact, a belated continuation of the Renaissance efforts to recover and reintegrate the world of classical Greek and Roman culture. The further the Winkelmann essay is divorced from the form and context of its periodical publication, the less its contemporary significance and urgency can be understood.

Why should we work towards an edition that represents the working Pater of, say, 1865 (when "Coleridge's Writing" was written) rather than the repentant Pater of 1889 (publication of *Appreciations*), or, more critically, why should we support the Hegelian Pater of 1866 (in the Winckelmann essay) rather than the respectful Pater of later versions of the Renaissance essays? Would such a banal chronological ordering of the essays imperil the positions of those – among whom I have even found myself – who have argued for the organic unity of works like *Studies in the History of the Renaissance* and *Appreciations*? My conclusion is that the organic unity for which we have argued remains. My point would be that the periodical versions of the essays represent an entirely different kind of order from that which Pater himself created in his revisions. In the first place, the 'order' of the individual books as they came out, and the slightly different 'order' of the posthumous Macmillan Library Edition, obscure the way in which Pater's thinking about remote historical epochs developed from his discovery of current or contemporary notions of history and the historical process. The order which I propose would demonstrate – almost in the form of a narrative – the full extent of his intellectual development of the late 'sixties and 'seventies. I believe such a publication would show the consistency and continuity of thought in a figure who is frequently criticized for inconsistency, and neglected for a supposed lack of intellectual rigour. The periodical publication of the essays, when compared with the revised later versions, shows Pater responding, like his contemporary Thomas Hardy, to the internal and external claims of Victorian society. In the disparity between the periodical and book publications we have an opportunity to observe the nature of what is 'permitted' and where. Pater's move from the relatively ephemeral *Westminster Review* or *Fortnightly Review* to eternal entombment on the shelves of the family library introduces us as much, I would guess, to the difference in audience as it does to Pater's inner changes of consciousness.

There is another issue that causes me to advocate publishing Pater's essays in the order and (apart from obvious oversights) in the form in which they originally appeared. The post-periodical essay collections are widely known as parts of organized books. These forms continue to be available and seem to have some appeal to commercial and scholarly presses. The periodical versions are much more difficult to acquire and inconvenient to use – unless your library has a collection of Victorian periodicals.

So it is not just that I believe that Pater will be more fully and more fairly represented by a carefully annotated publication of his essays in their periodical form. Such a publication would give scholars and students special access to the life of the period. As John North says in *Victorian Periodicals: A Guide to Research*:

> The Victorian age is the first for which we have as sensitive a record of a civilisation as the periodical press.[2]

Pater's part in that 'sensitive record' is insufficiently appreciated – too much of our work has been to show what Pater was *not*. An edition of his work highlighting the periodical essays might well change the table of contents even of the *Norton Anthology*.

SHARON BASSETT
California State University, Los Angeles

NOTES

1. Bruce Vardon, "Variant Readings in Walter Pater's *Studies in the History of the Renaissance*," Diss. University of Chicago 1950, p. li.
2. John S. North, "The Rationale – Why Read Victorian Periodicals?," *Victorian Periodicals: A Guide to Research*, ed. J. Don Vann and Rosemary T. Vanarsdel (New York: The Modern Language Association of America, 1978), p. 4.

Editing Walter Pater

Our would-be editor will probably want to replace the standard Library Edition (1910: reprinted 1967) with a scholarly edition that brings together all Pater's prose works, provides accurate and readable texts, and includes useful critical and textual notes. In preparing 'The Complete Prose Works of Walter Pater' he – like many specialists now contemplating the job of editing Victorian authors – will probably take as his model R. H. Super's definitive *The Complete Prose Works of Matthew Arnold* (1960-77), which, to quote a reviewer for the *TLS* (4 January, 1974), quickly "established itself as a centrepiece of modern Victorian scholarship."

This edition of Pater – based on a modification of Super's editorial procedures – will provide university students, teachers and general readers with all the information indispensable to an understanding of his literary achievement. Pater's letters will be excluded, and so will his poetry (some early poems are in John Sparrow's collection). It will reprint all the items in the Library Edition, together with the fugitive pieces identified by Arthur Symons in 1897 and later reprinted in *Uncollected Essays* (1903) and in *Sketches and Reviews* (1919), the review articles identified by Samuel Wright and Lawrence Evans, and the unpublished literary remains at Harvard, Oxford and elsewhere.

Now, Super printed Arnold's writings in the order of their first appearance – presumably to show whether his genius "progresses, evolves, or spins upon itself," as S. T. Coleridge says (6 August, 1832) in *Table Talk*. Reviewers, however, complained that this practice produced some extraordinary incongruities. Breaking up collections of essays, such as *Essays in Criticism*, First and Second Series, for example, forced Professor Super to invent fancy titles. One critic claimed that "twenty years from now there will be graduate students, and perhaps even professors of English, who are firmly persuaded that Arnold wrote a volume entitled *The Last Word*" (see *MP*, February 1980). The last word may well be Super's: "an author whose books include *Mixed Essays* and *Irish Essays and Others* was less interested in his titles than in getting his work before the public."

Our editor will probably object to this practice and resolve to make every effort to preserve the integrity of the volumes we have – especially those published during Pater's lifetime. Thus, he would argue, as C. L. Shadwell did in his Preface (1896) to *Gaston de Latour*, that no work of Pater's "should appear in a form less complete than he would himself have approved." After some reflection he will have to reconsider his position, for he will realise that Pater would never have authorised the publication of *Essays from 'The Guardian'*, the volume that Edmund Gosse prepared in an edition (1896) of 100 copies for "the inner circle of [Pater's] friends," and which was later included in the handsome *édition de luxe* and the Library Edition. As Symons pointed out in *The Athenaeum* (12 June, 1897), this book contains only a portion of Pater's literary journalism, and not the most important at that. All nine pieces originally appeared without Pater's signature. Our editor will have to face the fact that the posthumous publications, supervised by Gosse, Lionel Johnson and Shadwell, present extraordinary difficulties.

Let us say that *Greek Studies, Miscellaneous Studies* and *Gaston* were retained, but that *Essays from 'The Guardian'* gave way to a volume that included *all* of Pater's literary journalism and that the unpublished fragments made up the tenth and last volume: would this arrangement give us the Pater canon? Should our editor consider resurrecting, say, *Dionysus and Other Studies* and *Three Short Stories*, volumes which he worked on from 1874-8 and from 1890-2 respectively? Pater never explained why he stopped the publication of *Dionysus* – after Alexander Macmillan had advertised the book in the press, and had reassured Pater that it would make a worthy successor to *The Renaissance*. Nor did Pater explain why he prevented Macmillan from announcing that the book would not appear. Obviously he thought that it might one day. Perhaps a better case could be made for assembling *all* the uncollected portraits, which Pater preferred writing. Pater died with four published portraits uncollected and unpublished fragments of four more.

Our editor may well decide to print the essays, portraits and sketches in the order of their first appearance. The unpublished material will have to be dated as accurately as possible and inserted in the appropriate places. The tables of contents of the books Pater published will have to be included so that the reader can reconstruct them for himself. The volumes will have to be numbered, not titled.

This arrangement may damage the integrity of Pater's books slightly, but not as much as might be expected. Our editor would probably point out that, although Pater addressed himself to "a comparatively small section of readers" (letter of 11 November, 1872) at the outset of his career, he later turned his attention to reaching beyond literary and artistic circles to what he called "average readers" (letter of 1 November, 1892).

Determining the copy-text is no easy job either, because few manuscripts of Pater's works have survived and he incessantly revised his works – at first to remove grounds for misunderstanding and to avoid giving offence but later to clarify his views on aesthetics and ethics. Some alterations, like the suppression of the "Conclusion" from the second (1877) edition of *The Renaissance* and the suppression of "Aesthetic Poetry" from the second (1890) and subsequent editions of *Appreciations*, were perfectly obvious; others, like the thousands of changes made to *Marius*, were far too subtle to be noticed by his most careful readers, Shadwell included.

The text for most items will probably be based on the last version printed in Pater's lifetime. In determining Pater's final intention our editor will take as his guide the essay on "Style" (1888), which, as Ian Fletcher pointed out, served as his "aesthetic *credo*." (Pater considered the principles of this essay so important that he abandoned *Gaston* in 1888 and spent four years revising *Marius* for the third edition of 1892.)

According to this scheme, then, each volume will consist of (a) the Editor's Preface, (b) the Text, (c) Critical and Explanatory Notes, (d) Textual Notes and (e) a thorough Index. The Critical and Explanatory Notes, headed by a brief comment on the inception, composition and publication of the work in question, will identify Pater's allusions and quotations, and give the background of the work. The Textual Notes, introduced by bibliographic information that provides a history of the text, will indicate the most significant variant readings. Printers' errors – faulty punctuation, errors in dating, pagination, spelling and transposition – can be silently corrected. Pater's footnotes – properly identified – will appear at the bottom of the page.

Separating text, commentary and notes this way, relegating the commentary and the notes to a separate place at the back of each volume, will reduce the production cost considerably. Moreover, the text itself, free of the usual editorial apparatus, will be more readable than it would otherwise be.

Of course editing Pater – producing satisfactory texts of his work – is not as simple as these remarks might suggest. Nevertheless, before we can "deal critically with his work," to use the words of Fredson Bowers (*SAB*, 1970), we *must* determine as best we can precisely what he wrote and when. This project – the complete collection of Pater's prose – requires an editor of wide culture – he will have to be a textual scholar as well as a critical scholar – and a publisher of some means. It also needs the co-operation of Pater scholars everywhere.

R.M. SEILER
The University of Calgary

The "Paper in MS.": A Problem in Establishing the Chronology of Pater's Composition

In writing to Alexander Macmillan in June 1872, concerning the essays he was submitting for the volume on the Renaissance, Pater mentions, in addition to the five pieces that had appeared in the *Westminster Review* and the *Fortnightly Review*, that he is sending, as well, a "paper in MS." that "has not been published hitherto," which he does not further identify. In October, a spokesman for Macmillan writes to Pater that "the Essay you refer to was printed, but in deference to your wish it shall be cancelled." Pater apparently wanted to incorporate portions of the unnamed essay into the Preface he was composing for the volume: on 2 November, he writes to Macmillan: "I have not yet received the Preface and the rejected essay, which were to be returned to me for the alteration of the former."[1]

Lawrence Evans speculates that this unnamed "paper in MS." was a "first version of 'The School of Giorgione', whose extended theoretical passages enlarge on the doctrines of the Preface."[2] In his recent edition of *The Renaissance*, Donald Hill concurs in this judgement, although he speculates that the unpublished manuscript could have been any of the five hitherto unpublished essays that went into the first edition of *The Renaissance*.[3]

It seems that one cannot assume, with complete confidence, that Evans is correct in his supposition, without further documentary evidence, which appears to be unavailable. Indeed, one must assume that establishing a credible chronology of Pater's composition, in both the initial and revision stages, will be a most demanding task for the editors of the prospective new edition.

Professor Hill acknowledges Bruce Vardon's earlier effort at a scholarly edition of the 1873 version of *The Renaissance*.[4] Significantly, Vardon identifies this "paper in MS." as possibly a version of the essay on "Giordano Bruno," which was not published until August 1889, in the *Fortnightly Review*, and, after Pater's death, in somewhat expanded form as the seventh chapter of *Gaston de Latour*.

Faced with the great period of time between gestation and publication for the essay that Vardon's early identification necessitates, both Professor Evans and Professor Hill, not surprisingly, ignore their predecessor's note. In his brief account of the publication history of Pater's books during his lifetime, Robert Seiler assumes without comment that the essay on Bruno was written, along with the other eventually published five chapters, in the late 1880s, as the beginnings of a sequel to *Marius the Epicurean.*[5]

Implicitly, Seiler assumes as well that an essay on "the lower pantheism," as Pater calls the mystical philosophy of Bruno, is unlikely to have been even partially the product of the same period in Pater's life as the essays of *The Renaissance*, which have certainly as one of their overarching themes the liberating effect of 'pagan' moral and aesthetic values on a dualistic Christian culture.

Whether or not Vardon's tentative identification of the "paper in MS." is right is probably a point not susceptible of definitive judgment. Still, his thirty-year-old note exists, and the question of whether Pater's "paper in MS." concerns Giorgione or Giordano suggests that as we consider the problems and possibilities of a new edition we had better be very careful about small things.

I will not undertake to argue for the essay on Bruno over that on Giorgione as the probable "paper in MS." However, even a cursory reading of chapter seven of *Gaston* makes it seem as though Giordano's philosophy, as Pater construes it, constitutes an appropriate response to the view of experience expressed in the "Conclusion" to *The Renaissance*. And Pater's formulation of Bruno's view of the relation between "divine consciousness" and "human intelligence" bears a strong resemblance to Coleridge's theory of the primary and secondary imaginations. Recalling that Coleridge was very much on Pater's mind in the 1860s, one is tempted to find an apparently consonant idea in an essay supposedly not begun until the 1880s. Then, too, one of Pater's first major publications after the first edition of *The Renaissance* was his great essay on Wordsworth. Perhaps a lost draft of "Bruno" was written between 1866 and 1874.

One last thought on "Bruno" and the English Romantics: the "Imaginary Portrait" of "An English Poet," although not published until 1931, was probably written in the mid-1870s and contains several passages that are similar to the description of Bruno's "lower pantheism." Also, "An English Poet" contains some references to the principle of *Andersstreben*, central to the idea of form and matter that Pater presents in "Giorgione." The mutual concern of these two essays may imply a later dating for "Giorgione" than Professor Evans' speculative footnote suggests.

Of course, the essay on "Bruno" as published in 1889 shows us, not surprisingly, Pater in the early stages of thinking out the lectures that comprise *Plato and Platonism*. Nonetheless, three modest coincidences suggest, not altogether implausibly, the possible accuracy of Vardon's identification of the "paper in MS." as an early draft (or a completed version of a portion) of the essay on "Giordano Bruno."

First, Pater refers by name in the essay to Darwin, and much of his exposition of Bruno's theories turns upon "the evolution of things." One recalls that *The Descent of Man* was published in 1872, the same year as Pater's letter to Macmillan quoted above.

Second, Pater says that Bruno's philosophy "anticipates by a whole generation" the "Baconian philosophy of experience." Perhaps Bacon's rather abrupt entry into the essay may be related to the fact that James Spedding's monumental edition came out in a revision in 1870 (the first edition was 1857 and following).

Finally, Tennyson's "The Higher Pantheism" was published in 1869. Swinburne's devastating parody appeared in 1880. Does it seem likely that Pater, ever flinching from prospective criticism or ridicule, particularly in light of the abuse he received in Mallock's *New Republic* (1877) would have risked the phrase, "the lower pantheism," in the later 'seventies or the 'eighties if he had not committed himself to it before 1877?

These bits of information certainly do not 'prove' anything about the date of first composition of an essay on "Giordano Bruno." But they are suggestive that Vardon may have been right in guessing at an early rather than a late date.

Another point is that Pater plainly had sixteenth-century France on his mind when he composed the essay on du Bellay. While the focus of his early work, as Pater defines it in the "Preface," is on fifteenth-century Italy, it may well be that his studies and writing about the French Renaissance were fully underway, too, in the early 'seventies, only to be displaced in the mid-'seventies by the study of classical culture and myth, and then taken up, as having renewed relevance or promise, after the success of the first edition of *Marius*.

As Vardon's perusal of the record of Pater's borrowings from the Taylor Institution reveals, Pater was probably reading heavily in Michelet at the same time he was studying du Bellay's works, in late 1871 and early 1872.[6]

Why wouldn't he, under such stimulation as I have outlined, be as likely to produce an early version of an essay on Giordano Bruno as on Giorgione? The problem of the "paper in MS." seems not altogether solved, and that small problem, perhaps similar to many other textual problems in Pater's works, suggests the challenges that await the editors of the proposed new edition.

HAYDEN WARD
West Virginia University

NOTES

1. *Letters of Walter Pater*, ed. Lawrence Evans (Oxford: Oxford U.P., 1970), pp. 7-9.
2. *Letters*, p. 8.
3. *The Renaissance: Studies in Art and Poetry: The 1893 Text*, ed. Donald L. Hill (Berkeley: U. of California Press, 1980), p. 397.
4. Bruce E. Vardon, "Variant Readings in Walter Pater's *Studies in the History of the Renaissance*," Diss., University of Chicago, 1950, p. ii.
5. *Walter Pater: The Critical Heritage*, ed. R. M. Seiler (London: Routledge & Kegan Paul, 1980), p. 16.
6. Vardon, pp. 365-7.

Walter Pater Studies: 1970-1980

As Lawrence Evans pointed out in his contribution to *Victorian Prose: A Guide to Research* (ed. David J. DeLaura), the 1960s saw "a vigorous revival of scholarly and critical interest" in Walter Pater. He was the subject of no less than five books, twenty-five doctoral dissertations – according to the *Comprehensive Dissertation Index: 1861-1972* (1973) – and about thirty-five scholarly articles. Not surprisingly, this critical activity increased enormously during the 1970s. In the United States alone thirty-six doctoral dissertations on Pater were completed. And he was the subject of more than ten books and over seventy scholarly articles. This "revival" has been – as Evans put it – something of a mixed blessing "for those who value scholarly thoroughness and critical rigor." Many commentators have been – to paraphrase T.S. Eliot – interested, but not exactly in the subject before them; and are learned, but in something quite beside the point; many have extracted "something from their subject which is not fairly in it." Fortunately there are signs that things are changing. One is the *Pater Newsletter*, which was founded in 1977 to encourage co-operation and thus reduce duplication. Serious students of Pater will find it worth their while to subscribe: the Winter issue emanates from the University of Arizona at Tuscon (ed. Billie Andrew Inman), the Summer issue from the University College of Wales at Aberystwyth (ed. Laurel Brake). Another sign is the determined effort of a few commentators to produce a scholarly edition of Pater's works. The object of this (albeit brief and highly selective) survey is to draw attention to the work of those who have attempted to see the object as in itself it really is, which in Pater's case means establishing fundamental matters of fact.

I. Bibliography, Manuscripts and Editions

Pater bibliography is no longer in "uncharted wasteland," to use Evans' phrase. Indeed, specialists and non-specialists who wish to hack their way through the jungle of publications will find two guides helpful. One is Samuel Wright's *Bibliography of the Writings of Walter H. Pater* (1975), which lists in chronological order all of Pater's published and unpublished works, as well as the fugitive pieces, manuscripts and poetry. Wright deals with "the first English and American editions up to the date of the New Library Edition, 1910." This book also includes a number of valuable appendices, including notes on T.B. Mosher, who printed many of Pater's works in *The Bibelot*, and Mrs May Ottley's introduction to "Imaginary Portraits. 2. An English Poet," which appeared in the *Fortnightly Review*, 1931.

At present Wright is preparing an "Index to the Writings of Pater." He calls this work "an Informative Index, with short notes on all entries."

The other useful guide is *Walter Pater: An Annotated Bibliography of Writings about Him* (1980), which was edited by Franklin E. Court. It lists secondary material in chronological order – from the first review in 1871 to 1973. There are five indexes, including an authors and titles index. Contributors include Richard Bizot, Francis L. Nye, Lawrence Schreiber and Samuel Wright.

Regrettably, only a few manuscripts of Pater's published works have survived. A number of poems that he wrote in his youth, as well as lengthy and unedited portions of *Gaston de Latour* (1888) and the manuscript of "Demeter and Persephone" (1875) are in the collection of John Sparrow. (Sparrow is preparing an edition – with facsimiles – of the unfinished chapters of *Gaston*.) The manuscript of "Diaphaneitè" (1864) is at King's School, Canterbury, and that of "Pascal" (1894) at the Bodleian Library, Oxford. The rest, autograph letters, essays and fragments – "Literary and Scholarly Papers" (bMS. Eng. 1150) – are located in the Harvard College Library (see Wright's bibliography, 145-7, for a description of the items). Sharon Bassett, Department of English, California State University, Los Angeles, is preparing an edition of these pieces.

One fragment, "Arezzo" (1872?), probably transcribed by Clara Pater, describes the town of that name, as well as the tradition of art from which Michelangelo drew his inspiration. Laurel Brake argues in "A Commentary on 'Arezzo': An Unpublished Manuscript by Walter Brake" (*RES*, 1976) that Pater intended it to be a prelude to the essay on Michelangelo (1871) and that Pater withdrew it – not "The School of Giorgione" (1877), as Evans claims in his edition of *Letters of Walter Pater* (1970) – from *The Renaissance* (1873).

If undergraduates know Pater at all they probably know him as the author of *The Renaissance*. We have two new editions of this book, which until recently has been rather neglected by commentators. Evans' edition – issued by Pandora Books in 1977 – reprints the 1922 Macmillan edition; that is, it follows the 1893 edition, which is the last to have the benefit of Pater's supervision. "The School of Giorgione" is included. Evans' introduction is short but informative.

The scholarly edition that Donald L. Hill prepared for the University of California Press (1980) is, as David J. DeLaura says in the blurb on the dustjacket, "one of the most impressive works of Victorian scholarship" to appear in many years. Following the 1893 text, this edition provides two of Pater's book reviews (1872 and 1875), complete sets of Textual Notes, which record all the variant readings in the other editions, and Critical and Explanatory Notes, which give the history of the composition, publication and reception of each essay and identify Pater's allusions and quotations, together with an essay on the book as a whole, and seventeen illustrations. A paperback version of this important edition is also available.

The other works – especially in inexpensive reprints – are practically unobtainable. Osbert Burdett's Everyman edition (1934) of *Marius the Epicurean* (1885) and Eugene J. Brzenk's paperback collection (1964) of *Imaginary Portraits* (1887) have long been out of print. Of course, only "The Complete Prose Works of Walter Pater" will set the record straight. Perhaps the University of California Press can be persuaded to take up the project. C. W. Willerton, who prepared "A Study of Walter Pater's *Appreciations*" (Diss. South Carolina at Chapel Hill, 1979) might be invited to edit Pater's fourth book.

In the meantime, students and teachers will have to make do with two compact anthologies, namely Jennifer Uglow's *Walter Pater: Essays on Literature and Art* (1973) and Harold Bloom's *Selected Writings of Walter Pater* (1974). Jennifer Uglow has taken her material primarily from *The Renaissance* and *Appreciations* (1889): the pieces include "Coleridge's Writings" (1865), "Aesthetic Poetry" (1868), "Style" (1888), and "A Novel by Mr Oscar Wilde" (1891) and are arranged in four sections: The Youthful Ideal of Culture, The Dialectic Art, Critical Method, and Literary Criticism. This arrangement is supposed to enable the reader to appreciate the development of Pater's critical thought. All the essays (sixteen altogether) "reveal Pater's preoccupation with balance and harmony." The introduction is succinct but critically not as rigorous as it might be. The bibliographical information is slight, the notes just adequate.

Bloom's paperback edition (New American Library) reprints (twenty in all) selections – his favourites – from *The Renaissance, Imaginary Portraits, Plato and Platonism* (1893), *Greek Studies* (1895) and *Sketches and Reviews* (1919), together with "The Child in the House" (1878). The long introduction develops Bloom's thesis that Pater will prove "to be the valued precursor of a Post-Modernism still fated to be another last Romanticism." The bibliographical information and the notes are thorough.

II. Biography and Letters

The would-be biographer of Pater faces the challenge of grasping the character of a man who lived a singularly uneventful life, who never achieved great popularity during his lifetime and who, by design, discouraged an examination of his private life. He will be painfully aware of Arthur Symons' prophecy (1897) that no definitive life will ever appear.

The enterprising biographer will have to correct the distorted portraits produced by A. C. Benson in *Walter Pater* (1906) and Thomas Wright in *The Life of Walter Pater* (1907), as well as that produced by their close friend Edmund Gosse, who wrote the biographies for the *Contemporary Review* (December, 1894) and the *DNB* (1895 and 1909). As Laurel Brake points out in "Problems in Victorian Biography: The *DNB* and the

DNB 'Walter Pater' " (*MLR*, 1975), Pater's biographers differ profoundly in their explanations of Pater's estrangement from Benjamin Jowett, the powerful Master of Balliol College, Oxford. Benson, on the one hand, argued that Jowett identified Pater with the Aesthetic Movement or supposed that Pater's teachings encouraged a species of Hedonism or modern Paganism, and that Jowett made "it plain that he did not desire to see the supposed exponents of the aesthetic philosophy holding office in the University." Wright, on the other hand, claimed that Pater, hopelessly in the wrong, resolved to keep his wayward tongue under stricter control.

The truth of the matter, David Newsome tells us in *On the Edge of Paradise. A. C. Benson: the Diarist* (1980), is that "Jowett had gained possession of certain compromising letters which he had threatened Pater he would publish should he ever think of standing for university office." No wonder Pater avoided scandal like the plague. He had only to remember the fate that befell his contemporary, J. A. Symonds, who had to give up his fellowship (in 1862) after a number of his letters and poems were circulated among his colleagues. Phyllis Grosskurth says in *John Addington Symonds* (1964) that after he left Magdalen College, Oxford, Symonds was destined to spend the rest of his life as a semi-invalid, suffering from "acute anxiety neurosis."

Specialists will find Benson's diaries – altogether they run to 180 volumes or more than four million words – fascinating because, as Newsome observes, "Benson's career placed him at various stages of his life within the most eminent and influential circles of late Victorian and Edwardian England." Benson began recording his private thoughts about his friends and critics in the summer of 1897, when he was a housemaster at Eton College, and continued to do so until his death, as Master of Magdalene College, Cambridge, in June 1925.

One biography appeared in the 1960s – Germain d'Hangest's massive study (1961) of Pater's interior life. Two appeared in the 1970s – Gerald Monsman's *Walter Pater* (1977) and Michael Levey's *The Case of Walter Pater* (1978). Monsman's book, designed for "the general reader, the undergraduate, and the fledgling graduate student," focuses on the fiction – as autobiography – and the concept of the Aesthetic Hero. As expected – see his *Pater's Portraits: Mythic Pattern in the Fiction of Walter Pater* (1967) – Monsman sees Pater as a "modern mythmaker"; consequently, he minimises the significance of works like *Plato and Platonism*. (The reader would do well to consider as a supplement, say, I. C. Small's article, "Plato and Pater: Fin-de-Siècle Aesthetics" [*JBA*, 1972].) Monsman's monograph is nevertheless a useful introduction to Pater.

Now it is nothing new to read Pater's fiction as oblique autobiography. William Sharp – who got to know Pater quite well in the late 1880s – pointed out that Pater was "one of those authors of whom there can never be any biography away from his writings" (*Atlantic Monthly*, 1894). Levey, however, reads *all* of Pater's writings as oblique autobiography. The Director of the National Gallery bases his case for yet another biography on Pater's courageous struggle – all too often ignored by commentators – to rescue the appreciation of art from – to use Symons' words – "the dangerous moralities, the uncritical enthusiasm and pre- judices, of Mr. Ruskin." Levey sees Pater as a self-explorer who, in the process of recording the dialogue of his mind with itself, "encouraged the concept of personally scrutinizing a work of art."

The Case of Walter Pater is an engaging 'psychological' biography. Wherever possible Levey bases his inferences on facts (the first chapter in particular provides many new details about the Pater family). The portrait he produces, nevertheless, is unsubstantial, for he glides over such mat- ters as Pater's sources, aesthetic theories, religious position and influ- ences. However strange, this is a book that cannot be ignored.

Future biographers will likewise find useful R. M. Seiler's "Recollec- tions of Walter Pater," which, when completed, will bring together the impressions of about 100 people who knew him. Some of the material will be printed for the first time.

Recently, Cynthia Cirile and Herbert H. Lehman, H. Lehman College, discovered eleven letters that are not in *Letters of Walter Pater*: seven are to Oscar Browning, one to "Collier," one to T. H. Ward and two to F. W. Bussell. She also found thirty-seven letters from Richard C. Jackson to Browning. For information about Richard Charles Jackson, 1851-1923, see Samuel Wright's article in the *Antigonish Review*, 1971.

Two more 'finds' should be mentioned, namely George P. Landow's, which appeared in *N&Q* for October of 1975, and John C. Conlon's, which appeared in *N&Q* for August of 1978. Landow reprints Pater's letter dated 12 February [1877?] to Charles Rowley, the Manchester framemaker, Christian Socialist and author. Conlon reprints three letters dated 20 May [1882], 8 February, [1883] and [14 or 21 February 1883] to D. S. MacColl, a co-founder and co-editor of the *Oxford Magazine*. Pater's review of *Love in Idleness* appeared in the *Oxford Magazine* for 7 March, 1883.

III. General Studies

Some of the book-length general studies that purport to deal with the whole of Pater's literary career are disappointing indeed. Tentative think- ing, thesis 'pushing' and obscure writing mar much of the critical activity. Altogether they add very little to our knowledge of Pater.

David A. Downes's book, *The Temper of Victorian Belief* (1972), is a case in point. Like his first, *Victorian Portraits: Hopkins and Pater* (1965), this is another "comparative study of the minds and works of important Victorians." In the Preface Downes says that he has "tried to discuss the 'religious imagination' as essentially Romantic by examining the apological novels of Pater, Newman, and Kingsley in the context of the intellectual and spiritual temper of each as authentic Victorians." There is more than a little fogginess here. Elsewhere he talks of New- man's "dualistic dilemma of self and soul," and of history as "an elemental mode of the intellectualization of the total flux of events." Except for an interesting chapter on *Marius, The Temper of Victorian Belief* has little for the non-specialist. If he wishes to learn something about, say, the link between Newman and Pater he will have to read David J. DeLaura's authoritative book, *Hebrew and Hellene in Victorian England* (1969).

Or, if he has the stamina, Robert L. Wolff's *Gains and Losses* (1977). This massive book grew out of a publishing project that involved the reissue of 121 religious novels of the period for the Garland Reprint Series; it consists of plot summaries, biographical sketches and commentary – organised according to the appropriate denominational or theological point of view, i.e. from that of Dissenters, followers of the Church of England (Low, High and Broad) or non-believers. This Harvard historian is thorough, perhaps to a fault; his book is readable, but only in small portions. The image of Pater that emerges from the sections that are devoted to him is summarised thus: "[he] was a man of homosexual leanings and, paradoxically, while he was not a fully believing Christian, by the time he wrote *Marius* he was once more a ritualist, as he had been in his boyhood."

Another work that exhibits tentative thinking and obscure writing is Richard L. Stein's *The Ritual of Interpretation* (1975). This book purports to examine "the Victorian literature of art [i.e. fiction and poetry, together with autobiographical and critical prose] in terms of the three practitioners of the genre – John Ruskin, Dante Gabriel Rossetti, and Walter Pater," with a view to understanding not only Victorian aesthetics but also the place of aesthetics in the development of the age. His thesis – Stein is often guilty of thesis 'pushing' – is that "the act of interpretation" in their writings takes on an "almost religious value." He also says that "the contemplation of art under the guidance of literature is endowed with an almost magical power to transform the being of the spectator." As he puts it in the Introduction, "The ritual quality of the styles of all three writers forces the reader to experience the contemplation of art as an all-consuming act, one that can involve a fundamental re-orientation of the self." The reader will find this heady stuff indeed.

Two more works merit brief mention. One is Richard Wollheim's *On Art and the Mind* (1973), an attractive collection of essays and lectures that explores the ways that the philosophy of mind and the philosophy of art interact. This philosopher has included a paper on Pater and metaphysics that will interest Pater specialists in particular; it tries to overthrow the prevailing notion of Pater as an aesthete by showing how his theoretical remarks have been misunderstood.

The other is Peter A. Dale's *The Victorian Critic and the Idea of History* (1977), a work which will interest literary historians especially. Dale argues that Carlyle, Arnold and Pater were preoccupied with "the historical process and its philosophical meanings"; they studied history so that they could understand the development of the human spirit. Pater is the focal point of the book. He shows how Pater's historicism sprang from a mixture of Romantic attitudes and positivistic ideas.

IV. Special Studies

These studies – primarily articles – also vary in thoroughness and critical rigour, as a cursory glance at the most characteristic pieces will show. Too often old ground is re-worked to little effect.

Criticism

Two articles take up a matter – Pater and the function of criticism – which for many specialists Graham Hough and Geoffrey Tillotson put to rest in, respectively, *The Last Romantics* (1949) and *Criticism and the Nineteenth Century* (1951). The first is Christopher Ricks's "Pater, Arnold and mis-quotation" (*TLS*, 25 November, 1977), which is as much an attack on "aesthetic criticism" as it is an attack on critics like Harold Bloom who refuse to admit (unlike Matthew Arnold) that " 'the critical faculty is lower than the inventive.' " Serious Paterians will remember that T. S. Eliot in "Hamlet" (1919) spoke of "that most dangerous type of critic [i.e. Walter Pater]: the critic with a mind that is naturally of the creative order, but which through some weakness in creative power exercises itself in criticism instead." These words also apply to Bloom, "an unrecon-structed re-constructing Paterian," who said in his introduction to the *Selected Writings of Walter Pater* that Pater's "writings obscure the sup-posed distinction between criticism and creation. ... 'Supposed', because who can convince us of that distinction?" The point of Ricks's attack is that "Arnold's modest shrewdness about the function of criticism leads him to quote impeccably, while Pater's quasi-creative arrogation misleads him to misquote peccably." Characteristically, Ricks claims, "each man overkills the thing he overloves."

In "Pater's Impressionism Reconsidered" (*ELH*, 1977) Paul Zietlow argues that Pater's "impressionistic critical method" – which pervades all his writings – is not a mere "second creation" or "aesthetic equivalent" for his sense of a work of art. Rather, "Fertilized by the energies in what he witnesses, [Pater] creates and evokes through his writing a sense of revived life, giving new shape to the old vitalities, and assisting in the resurrection and transmission of culture."

Much more illuminating is I. C. Small's "The Vocabulary of Pater's Criticism and the Psychology of Aesthetics" (*BJA*, 1978). Small traces the critical terms and concepts that Pater used in the "Preface" and "Conclusion" of *The Renaissance – impression, pleasurable moments, pleasurable sensations, relative* and *discriminate* – to the debate over "the physiology and psychology of aesthetics" conducted by Herbert Spencer, Alexander Bain and James Sully during the period 1860 to 1876.

Fiction

Ever since T. S. Eliot in 1930 dismissed *Marius* as a "hodge-podge" critics by the score have tried to show that Pater's fiction has an imagistic, dramatic or thematic pattern. The best book-length study remains Gerald Monsman's *Pater's Portraits*, notwithstanding his latest attempt to see Pater as mythographer. In *Walter Pater's Art of Autobiography* (1980) Monsman teases out of *Marius* and other works the theory that, whatever his subject, Pater meditated on the deaths of his parents and that, as a consequence, he foreshadows Deconstructionism. This phenomenonalizing of Pater – an interesting but reductive business – will primarily interest specialists.

Typical of the struggle to say something new is Lawrence F. Schuetz's "Pater's *Marius*: The Temple of God and the Palace of Art" (*ELT*, 1972), also the title of his Ph. D. dissertation (University of Wisconsin-Milwaukee, 1974). Schuetz claims that "the basic structural pattern of the novel is provided by Marius' re-enactment of the Cupid-Psyche myth." That is, Marius is not "an abstract Dionysian figure" but "a unique *anima* who retains his individual identity in re-enacting the archetypal quest of the human soul for union with the divine Ideal, here made more difficult by a period of social, cultural and religious upheaval."

Once again, the student would do well to consider a much more useful work, namely Robert T. Lenaghan's "Pattern in Walter Pater's Fiction" (*SP*, 1961), a work to which writers like Gerald Monsman are deeply indebted. Lenaghan sees the Dionysian-Apollonian tension as the principle that informs all Pater's fiction.

Sources, Backgrounds, Contexts

Some significant work has been done in these areas. I. C. Small has identified two sources for Pater's allusions to Spinoza in "Sebastian van Storck" (*N&Q*, 1978). The first is Andala's *Apologia pro vera & saniore philosophiae* ... (1719), which was a rarity even in the 1880s. Small believes that Pater knew the work – he probably read Ingram Bywater's copy – and that Pater was interested in Andala's "comparison between Spinoza's work and Stoicism." The other is John Colerus' *Life of Spinosa* (1706), the most important source of biographical information. Frederick Pollock had recently reprinted this work in his *Spinoza: His Life and Philosophy* (1880). Apparently "all of Pater's appropriations from Spinoza can be found within five pages of Pollock's work."

A work that will be warmly received – because at last some one can study Pater's reading – is Billie Andrew Inman's *Walter Pater's Reading: An Annotated Bibliography of His Library Borrowings and Literary References* (1981), which lists Pater's borrowings from Queen's College Library, the Bodleian Library, the BNC Library and the Taylor Institution Library for the period 1860-94. This work also lists the books from Pater's own library.

Influence

In the Introduction to his *Oxford Book of Modern Verse* (1936), W. B. Yeats said that Pater was the one writer who had the "entire uncritical admiration" of his generation. Just how *The Renaissance* and *Marius* 'dominated' the writers who established their reputations during the 1880s – and the 1890s – is still a matter for debate.

Gerald Monsman, in "Pater and His Younger Contemporaries" (*VN*, 1975), studies the impact that these works, particularly the "Conclusion" to *The Renaissance*, had on Yeats and the poets of the Rhymers' Club, Ezra Pound, Wallace Stevens, Henry James, Joseph Conrad, Virginia Woolf, James Joyce and T. S. Eliot. Monsman produces a catalogue of 'parallel' passages and direct and indirect acknowledgements; what is missing from such statements as "Stylistically the early Yeats out-Paters Pater" is the sense of indebtedness. He concludes: 'If one looks, one can find in Pater's ideal of the gem-like flame ... many fugitive threads out of which our present literature is woven." One should compare this article with John Pick's "Divergent Disciples of Walter Pater" (*Thought*, 1948), which looks at Pater's influence on Oscar Wilde, George Moore, Arthur Symons and Lionel Johnson.

In "Pater, Hopkins, and the Self" (*VN*, 1974), Gerald Monsman examines Pater's influence on Hopkins. (During the Trinity Term of 1866 Hopkins took his essay to Pater for criticism. They remained friends until September of 1879, when Hopkins left Oxford.) According to Monsman, the relationship "between the moral iconoclast and the priest who sacrificed so much for the sake of his religious scruples would be puzzling were it not for certain common metaphysical preoccupations that united them." Hopkins' interest in "inscape," Monsman argues, "seems inescapably linked to Pater's metaphysics of the self."

Jerome Bump in "Hopkins, Pater, and Medievalism" (*VN*, 1976) claims that Monsman's "emphasis on the similarity of Hopkins and Pater" obscures "the dialectical nature of their relationship." According to Bump, "If we are to focus on Pater's influence on Hopkins at Oxford we should consider one of the prime attractions of those years: Victorian medievalism, the source of many of their apparent affinities in aesthetics, metaphysics, and religion." This approach reveals that Hopkins opposed his tutor "in the continual debate between Hellenism and Hebraism" because Pater attempted "to make medievalism a vehicle for paganism."

Two of the most rewarding studies of Pater's influence have to be Richard Bizot's "Pater and Yeats" (*ELH*, 1976) and Perry Meisel's *The Absent Father: Virginia Woolf and Walter Pater* (1980). Bizot surveys the scholarship devoted to their literary relations, 'roughs out' a history of their relationship, and examines Pater's essay on Leonardo da Vinci, a key passage of which occupied Yeats's interest towards the close of his career. It will be remembered that Yeats maintained that only by printing the *Mona Lisa* passage in *vers libre* as he did in *The Oxford Book of Modern Verse* could he "show its revolutionary importance."

In *The Absent Father* Meisel tries to break through Woolf's silence on the subject of Pater – "there is no single essay about him nor any significant discussion of his work to be found anywhere in Woolf's writing" – and explore the influence that her reading of Pater and her studying (1898-1905) with his sister Clara had on her criticism and fiction. It was Wyndham Lewis in *Men Without Art* (1934) who first observed that the connection was much closer than most people suppose. The discipleship here is "a veiled and secret one." Just as she rejected the patriarchal influence of her father, Leslie Stephen, she rejected, neutralised and sublimated the influence of Pater. Meisel shows that "Woolf betrays her indebtedness to Pater by the recurrent and habitual use of particular figures of speech borrowed from the decisive moments in Pater's own vision."

Reputation

A clear picture of Pater's early reputation is beginning to emerge. R.M. Seiler's *Walter Pater: The Critical Heritage* (1980) provides a critical profile of Pater's reputation during the period 1873 to 1911, when P.E. More's attack on "Paterism" in the *Nation* (13 April, 1911) signalled a change in intellectual fashion. Contributors include Arthur Symons, George Eliot, Havelock Ellis, George Moore, Oscar Wilde, Edmund Gosse, Henry James, and Lionel Johnson.

Franklin E. Court's *Pater and His Early Critics* has been recently published as a monograph by the University of Victoria Press, British Columbia. This work is a study of a select number of responses to Pater's writings. Critics and reviewers discussed include Edmund Gosse, Mrs Oliphant and John Morley.

Specialists who are interested in Pater's later reputation, particularly the attempts of recent years to 'rehabilitate' him, will find Richard Wollheim's review article "The artistic temperament" (*TLS*, 22 September, 1978) stimulating. Wollheim arranges the critical thought about Pater on a spectrum that consists of "traditional" at one end and "revisionist" at the other. Lord David Cecil's lecture (1955) on Pater serves as the most succinct statement of the first school of criticism.

Style

Violet Paget believed that she could determine the essential peculiarities of Pater's "temperament and modes of being" at any given time by studying the style of a passage that he was writing (see "The Handling of Words: A Page of Walter Pater," *Life & Letters*, 1933). Interestingly enough, Gerald Monsman and Samuel Wright, in "Walter Pater: Style and Text" (*SAQ*, 1972), carefully study a passage that Pater re-wrote at various times during his literary career, namely the "Conclusion" to *The Renaissance*, which appeared in four versions over a period of twenty-five years. The image that emerges is that of a "timid" but stubborn Pater who refused to abandon his original meaning.

Studies of Individual Works

Finally, *The Renaissance* and the on-going debate over why the "Conclusion" was suppressed from the second edition.

Two essays throw new light on this book. Billie Andrew Inman, in "Pater's Conception of the Renaissance: From Sources to Personal Ideal" (*VN*, 1975), illustrates how the ideas that Pater borrowed from Jules Michelet and Jacob Burckhardt form "the basic lines" of his vision of the Renaissance, a vision which he formed in the 1860s. In "Walter Pater's *Renaissance* and Leonardo da Vinci's Reputation in the Nineteenth Century" (*MLR*, 1979) Barrie Bullen shows that Pater was "familiar with the new French interpretation of the painter's life and work," especially that of Stendhal, Michelet, Gautier, Rio, Clément and Houssaye. Bullen argues that Pater "and Gautier see the paintings of Leonardo as experiments in mental analysis, the projection in two dimensions of complexity and ambiguity beyond the reach of words."

For some time now specialists have believed that Pater omitted the "Conclusion" from the second edition (1877) of *The Renaissance* because he was sensitive to adverse criticism – particularly W.H. Mallock's satiric portrait of him as Mr Rose, the "aesthete," in *The New Republic*, which first appeared late in 1876 – and concerned about his reputation at Oxford.

Lawrence F. Schuetz claims in "The Suppressed 'Conclusion' to *The Renaissance* and Pater's Modern Image" (*ELT*, 1974) that "Neither view affords a very favourable image of Pater, and neither accords proper significance to his stated motive for withdrawing the piece." (Pater printed the "Conclusion," together with a note explaining his 'motives,' in the third edition, 1888.) Schuetz argues that Pater was motivated by "high seriousness" and "not by the weakness of character implied by the widely accepted views." What influenced Pater's decision in his opinion was John Wordsworth's letter of 17 March, 1873, and Pater's failure to obtain the Junior Proctorship at Oxford in 1874.

When "Pater's action is seen in the light of other contemporary evidence," Ian Small points out in "Pater and the Suppressed 'Conclusion' to *The Renaissance*: Comment and Reply" (*ELT*, 1976), Schuetz's "interpretation of that action [appears] much less plausible." Small, of course, refers to the articles in *The Oxford and Cambridge Undergraduates Journal*, containing allegations of "effeminacy," paganism and homosexuality that appeared – early in 1877 – while Pater was preparing the second edition and while he was trying for the Professorship of Poetry at Oxford. (Even outside Oxford Pater was known as a pagan: see *The World* for 31 January, 1877.) Surely, he concludes, "men less sensitive to criticism than Pater would have done the same."

Alan W. Bellringer takes the same view, namely that "In 1888 Pater was nervous of censure on the ground that his ideas perverted virtue into hedonism," in "The 'Conclusion' to *The Renaissance*: Pater's Original Meaning" (*PSt.* 1977). He compares the first version of the text, that is, the concluding paragraphs of "Poems by William Morris," which appeared in the *Westminster Review* (October 1868), with the four versions that appeared in the period 1873-93. The general tendency of the many changes Pater made in wording, Bellringer argues, "is to reduce the shock and offence which the original version gave to contemporary moral and religious opinion."

R.M. SEILER
University of Calgary

For Product Safety Concerns and Information please contact our EU
representative GPSR@taylorandfrancis.com
Taylor & Francis Verlag GmbH, Kaufingerstraße 24, 80331 München, Germany

www.ingramcontent.com/pod-product-compliance
Lightning Source LLC
Chambersburg PA
CBHW050458110726
47899CB00003B/992